HENRY TIMROD

HENRY TIMROD

A Biography

Walter Brian Cisco

Madison • Teaneck
Fairleigh Dickinson University Press

Associated University Presses
2010 Eastpark Boulevard
Cranbury, NJ 08512

The paper used in this publication meets the requirements of the American National Standard for Permanence of Paper for Printed Library Materials Z39.48–1984.

Library of Congress Cataloging-in-Publication Data

Cisco, Walter Brian, 1947-
    Henry Timrod : a biography / Walter Brian Cisco.
        p. cm.
    Includes bibliographical references and index.
    ISBN 0-8386-4041-9 (alk. paper)
1. Timrod, Henry, 1828–1867. 2. Poets, American—19th century—Biography.
3. South Carolina—Intellectual life—19th century. 4. South Carolina—
Biography. I. Title.
    PS3073.C575 2004
    811'.3—dc22

                                                    2004001338

For Jameson

Contents

Acknowledgments

Thanks are due the staffs of the following institutions: the University of South Carolina's South Caroliniana Library and the Thomas Cooper Library Interlibrary Loan Department; the South Carolina Department of Archives and History; South Carolina Historical Society; the Charleston Library Society; Special Collections Library, Duke University; Southern Historical Collection, University of North Carolina; Alderman Library, University of Virginia; Milton S. Eisenhower Library, Johns Hopkins University; Harry Ransom Humanities Research Center, University of Texas at Austin; Department of Rare Books and Special Collections, Princeton University; and Manuscripts and Archives Section, New York Public Library.

Among past Timrod scholars who deserve recognition are Guy A. Cardwell, Jr.; Jay B. Hubbell; and Edd Winfield Parks. I know what it means "to stand on the shoulders of giants."

HENRY TIMROD

Fig. 1. Timrod Memorial, Washington Park, Charleston.
(Henry T. Thompson, *Henry Timrod: Laureate of the Confederacy*)

Fig. 2. Henry Timrod, 1855 or 1856. Daguerreotype by Tyler & Company, Charleston. (South Caroliniana Library)

Fig. 3. Henry Timrod, c. 1861. The poet gave this photograph to
Rachel Lyons. (Timrod Memorial Association, *Proceedings*)

Fig. 4. Henry Timrod, 1863. Miniature photograph made for a locket. (South Caroliniana Library)

Fig. 5. Henry Timrod, 1867. Photograph by Wearn & Hix, Columbia.
(Timrod Memorial Associations, *Proceedings*)

1

"That boy will, if he lives, be a poet"

"JUST AS THE SUN OF A GLORIOUS MAY DAY WITH RAYS ASLANT WAS pointing down into the west, gilding each spire anew and touching the new mantles of grasses and trees with light, a shaft of fire invaded a bright enclosure near Charleston's beautiful City Hall and illuminated a scene of rare beauty." The *News and Courier* reporter used his most evocative language to describe an uncommon event. The crowd in Washington Park that spring afternoon in 1901 gathered to dedicate a monument in remembrance of, not a statesman or war hero, but a humble poet. As the bells of St. Michael's Church sounded the hour of five o'clock the proceedings began. William A. Courtenay, former mayor of the city, presided. The invocation was given by the Right Reverend Ellison Capers, Episcopal Bishop of South Carolina. Speechmaking would commence later. First came the unveiling. Mayor J. Adger Smyth released a ribbon and the huge United States flag covering the monument was pulled away. Atop a tall pedestal of Winnsboro gray granite was a larger-than-life bronze bust, executed by sculptor Edward V. Valentine. Amid cheers and applause children stepped forward with wreaths, bouquets, and floral tributes. Soon the base of the monument disappeared under a mound of roses, violets, pansies, sweet peas, and carnations. There was one magnificent arrangement of lilies and yellow roses in the form of a lyre.[1] The symbolism would have brought a smile to Henry Timrod.

🙚 🙚 🙚

One feature even the most skilled sculptor could not hope to capture in bronze. Yet through primitive lenses—in four photographic

19

exposures—the poet is revealed by his eyes. Sitting for a portrait in mid-1850s Charleston is a confident young man, filled with promise. Timrod's gray eyes, remembered a friend, "though slightly melancholy in repose, flashed with excitement and sparkled with mirth under their long curling lashes." Secession and war changed everything. In 1861 Timrod's fame as a poet soared, as did the hopes of fellow Confederates. His countenance then seems to glow with quiet pride. Two years later a weariness is evidenced in eyes dimmed by the continued carnage and his own physical decline. Faith in the justness of his country's cause could not stave off defeat. Stricken with poverty, grief, and a hopeless disease, the poet still strove to endure. From Timrod's final photograph, taken just months before his death, stare the eyes of one who has suffered too much.

﷼ ﷼ ﷼

Heinrich Dimroth was born near Kusel, a Rhineland town on the west bank of the Glan River, near the border of that confederation of principalities and duchies called the Holy Roman Empire. Encouraged by the British government, German immigrants began arriving in the South Carolina colony as early as the 1730s, settling in Orangeburg Township and in the city of Charleston. Dimroth was one of those who made the journey, probably arriving around 1765,[2] joining the thriving German community in Carolina's coastal metropolis.

He soon Anglicized his name to Henry Dimrod—and then Henry Timrod—but would not entirely abandon his ethnic heritage. Timrod was active in the newly founded *Deutscher Freundschaftbund* (German Friendly Society), one of several Charleston social and benevolent organizations. He borrowed 100 pounds from the Society, perhaps to launch his business as shoemaker and tailor, and in two years had repaid the debt with interest. Over the next two decades Timrod would serve the association as clerk, warden, vice president, and president. He also joined the congregation of St. John's Lutheran Church, worshipping in their wooden sanctuary on Archdale Street.[3]

Life in the new land was often difficult. Charlestonians of Timrod's generation suffered fires, floods, and fever; but they endured. Immigrants continued to arrive from England, Ireland, Scotland, the British West Indies, Germany, and the Netherlands. French Huguenots and Sephardic Jews found religious freedom and economic opportunity. The city spilled beyond its ancient protective walls. By 1761 the population stood at 8,000, evenly divided between slave and free. Charleston found itself at the center of a natural system of inland waterways—rivers and tidal creeks that brought rice, indigo, deerskins, and naval stores to the harbor for export.

The royal governor was commander-in-chief of all His Majesty's troops in the colony—regulars as well as militiamen.[4] The king's German subjects did their part by mustering the German Fusileers Military Company. But over the years loyalties would change as colonial grievances mounted. On the eve of the Revolutionary War the governor fled to a British warship as the South Carolina militia went over to the patriot cause. Henry Timrod joined the Fusileers as an orderly sergeant and saw duty in Charleston, Port Royal, and Savannah. The unit was disbanded when Charleston fell to the British in 1780.[5] Many would again pledge their allegiance, if not their true loyalty, to George III. After two years and seven months of bitter civil war in the South Carolina backcountry, the Redcoats finally evacuated.

With American independence won, Charleston flourished as never before. Her population doubled in but one generation. Ships lined the Cooper River wharves as cargo was transferred to and from Bay Street warehouses. In open-air markets vendors sold meat, fresh fish, vegetables, and fruit. Customers thronged King Street's shops and stores. Henry Timrod prospered as well. By now a middle-aged man, he resided in the city, served as an elder in the Lutheran Church, and still worked as a tailor. He had also purchased farm land near Parker's Ferry on Charleston Neck, that narrow stretch of the peninsula between the Cooper and Ashley rivers. He came to spend much of his time there.[6]

Little is known of Timrod's personal and family life. He had been married first to a widow named Mary White. After her death Mary's children by a previous marriage inherited her estate. He then married Christiana Hoff, also a widow, in January 1783. When she died in October 1784 Timrod waited but five months before marrying a third time. The *Gazette of the State of South-Carolina* reported that on Saturday night, March 19, 1785, the tailor was married "to his amiable housekeeper, Miss Susannah Hargan, lately arrived from the northwards."[7]

The bride was said to be first-generation Scots-Irish, Presbyterian, "a lady of extraordinary talent," according to a granddaughter. "Indeed whatever cleverness her children possessed, they believed to have been derived from her." Seven years after Susannah's marriage—on July 15, 1792—a son was born at their farm on Charleston Neck. His parents named him William Henry Timrod. Young William would have no memory of his father. Henry Timrod the elder died at his Parker's Ferry home on August 12, 1794.[8]

We do not know how many children survived, but William had at least one sister. Susannah Timrod had a difficult time supporting them. She was to have inherited one-third of the estate; the children two-thirds. By one account she soon remarried, "a step by which the family means, already reduced . . . were still further squandered." As late as 1809 a Charleston tobacco store operated under Henry Timrod's name, perhaps an enterprise carried on by his widow. William's daughter recounted a tradition that her father and his sister when young "resided in ease and plenty on their own plantation." But that house on Charleston Neck burned one night in 1795. All of their belongings—and property records—were lost. The heirs of Mary White Timrod were said to have successfully challenged Susannah's claim to the land.[9]

An entry in the minutes of the German Friendly Society for January 1802, when William was nine years old, grants that "the two youngest children of the late Henry Timrod be allowed not exceeding thirty pounds per year and that to be under the direction of the Committee on Charities." His daughter insisted that he was not taught at a public "free school," but rather he "was one of the pupils of Dr. Bess who kept then one of the best schools in Charleston." In any case, the boy's formal education would be brief.

William was an unusually bright child and loved to read. Unfortunately, the fire that destroyed their home had consumed the elder Timrod's substantial library. His mother cherished a dream of William becoming a lawyer, but according to a family story he found a way to thwart her plan. At the age of eleven he convinced himself that a bookbinder had, by the very nature of his work, unlimited access to the printed word. Insisting that his mother apprentice him to such a firm, he even ran away from home to make his point. Finally the child had his way,[10] though he quickly learned that the binding of books left little opportunity for the examination of their contents.

William's daughter later said he had "neither much time given him in the day to read, nor light at night." Still, he refused to be deterred. When the moon was bright William would climb to the roof, "there by the lunar rays to read into the small hours of the night. Shakespeare was at that time his favorite companion."[11] In addition to the study of literature, Timrod learned well his chosen trade, worked hard, and became a respected member of the community. In 1812 he bought the bookbindery at 25 Broad Street that had been operated by John and Benjamin Crow. He began to write poetry, and in 1814 published a small volume of seventy-eight pages entitled *Poems on Various Subjects*.[12]

Fellow Charleston businessman James McCarter—owner of a King Street bookstore—one summer entrusted Timrod with the operation of his affairs. "On my return, I rec^d from him a faithful and accurate account of every dollar received and disbursed by him. . . . In 1826 my business having enlarged, I persuaded him to move his bindery to my premises, and soon after his family followed his shop, and for seven or eight years, save during the summer, I was in daily if not hourly communication with him, as his Bindery was in the Kitchen part of my premises, and his family occupied the upper part of my house." McCarter had little appreciation for poetry, but was impressed by Timrod's work ethic. The bookbinder would labor all night, if necessary, rather than be late with an assignment. "I never knew so *faithful*, so *punctual*, so *conscientious*, a mechanic."

Charlestonians with literary interests would congregate at Timrod's bindery, among them George S. Bryan, William Gilmore Simms, James Louis Petigru, and Rev. Samuel Gilman. "Timrod's Club" was the name McCarter gave the group. "His wonderful powers of conversation, his genial manner, his pleasant and amiable temper, his exquisite humour, and pungent wit, soon gathered round him a knot of clever young men, who relished his company, and enjoyed his jokes. . . . There was no cessation of work when these distinguished gentlemen came to see him. With his coat off, his sleeves rolled up, and his apron on, he continued his occupation, without apology. He had that true dignity, and independence, which scorned to make apologies or to ask indulgence from men, who seemed so much higher in the social scale."[13] Admired for his intellect, Timrod yet remained what was called in those days a "mechanic." Social isolation was due as much to his own meager resources as to any constraints imposed by class-conscious Charleston. A daughter later explained that Timrod often refused invitations simply because "his means were far too cramped even to permit him to return any hospitality." Still, he seemed content. "I know that my father," she wrote, "like his children acknowledged no aristocracy but the aristocracy of genius."[14]

On December 19, 1812—less than a year after going into business for himself—William Timrod married Thyrza E. Prince. She was perhaps sixteen or seventeen years old, he twenty. "The perfection of her face and form caught his fancy," wrote a daughter, "the perfection of her character won and kept his heart through twenty-six years of married life." Thyrza was the daughter of Charles Prince, a devout Methodist whose parents had migrated from Somersetshire, England before the Revolution. Her mother was Sarah, daughter of John Rudolph Faesch, a Swiss immigrant and another veteran of the German Fusileers. According to family tradition Cardinal Joseph Fesch, Napoleon's uncle and ardent Bonepartist, was a relation.[15]

The couple may have lost children prematurely, a tragedy all too common. William's and Thyrza's first child for whom we have a record, Rebecca Adeline, was not born until 1823—over ten years after their marriage. Emily was born in 1827 and Edith Caroline in 1833. As she grew older Edith is said to have expressed herself in verse, though no example survives. "Rebecca was a saint," remembered one. Sister Emily called her "the most perfect character I ever knew." This eldest daughter was born crippled. Her father would write five loving, if didactic, stanzas encouraging her to rise above the handicap.[16] By all accounts she did.

William and Thyrza Timrod's only son was born in the family's living quarters above the bindery, between eleven and twelve o'clock on the evening of December 8, 1828. His father named him Henry H. Timrod, after his grandfather. The middle initial "H"—soon dropped—may have stood for grandmother Susannah's maiden name, Hargan.[17] The family would call him Henry, Harry, or simply Hal.

By the time his son was a toddler William Henry Timrod wrote a poem for the boy. The father's pedestrian versifying might be unremembered but for his subject—and for the third stanza's dark prophecy.

To Harry

Harry, my little blue-eyed boy,
    I love to hear thee playing near;
There's music in thy shouts of joy
    To a fond father's ear.

I love to see the lines of mirth
    Mantle thy cheek and forehead fair,
As if all pleasures of the earth
    Had met to revel there;

For gazing on thee, do I sigh
    That these most happy hours will flee,
And thy full share of misery
    Shall fall in life on thee!

There is no lasting grief below,
    My Harry! that flows not from guilt;
Thou can'st not read my meaning now -
    In after times thou wilt.

Thou'lt read it when the churchyard clay
    Shall lie upon thy father's breast,
And he, though dead, will point the way
    Thou shalt be always blest.

They'll tell thee this terrestrial ball,
    To man for his enjoyment given,
Is but a state of sinful thrall
    To keep the soul from heaven.

My boy! the verdure-crowned hills,
    The vales where flowers innumerous blow,
The music of ten thousand rills
    Will tell thee, 'tis not so.

God is no tyrant who would spread
    Unnumbered dainties to the eyes,
Yet teach the hungering child to dread
    That touching them he dies!

No! all can do his creatures good,
          He scatters round with hand profuse—
The only precept understood,
          "Enjoy, but not abuse!"[18]

Young Hal's world naturally revolved around his mother, and he was devoted to her. She cherished her children, and shared with them the simple pleasure and wonder she found in nature. The crowded city confined her spirit. "A walk in the woods to her was food and drink," remembered Emily, "and the sight of a green field gave her joy inexpressible." Thyrza Timrod's love of nature was exceeded only by her gift of observation. "From my childhood," continued Emily, "I can remember her love for flowers and trees and the stars. How she would call our attention to the glinting of the sunshine through the leaves of the trees, to the afternoon's light and shadow as they slept quietly together side by side, and even to a streak of moonlight on the floor. She would sit absorbedly watching the wavings of the branches of the trees in the wind and say, 'Don't they seem to be whispering to each other in a language of their own.'"

One day when Hal was four years old, he and his mother watched spellbound as lightning split the sky and thunder crashed outside the upstairs window of their Charleston home. His father was nearby. The little boy was clearly in awe of the storm's display of power.

"Mama," he said, "God is opening His great mouth and listen to His voice as it comes forth!"

"Thyrza," said William thoughtfully, "that boy will, if he lives, be a poet."[19]

2

"Blue skies above me, but a mist ahead"

IN THE YEAR THAT HENRY TIMROD WAS BORN CONGRESS PASSED WHAT
came to be known as the "Tariff of Abominations." Southerners
protested as average import duties were hiked to fifty percent, forc-
ing consumers to buy manufactured goods from Northern produc-
ers. The result of this protectionism, declared South Carolina College president Thomas Cooper, was "to sacrifice the south to the
north, by converting us into colonists and tributaries." The time was
fast approaching, he insisted, for Southerners to "calculate the value
of our union; and to inquire of what use to us is this most unequal al-
liance?" Other voices joined his. Some came to advocate secession.
Vice President of the United States John C. Calhoun was one South
Carolinian who sought to both preserve the Union and protect
Southern rights. He proposed that a state might nullify (suspend
within its borders the enforcement of) an offending Federal law. If
later overruled by a three-fourths majority of all the states, the ag-
grieved state could either acquiesce, or then choose secession.

Most South Carolinians would embrace Calhoun's strategy. In the
fall of 1832 a Convention of the People met in Columbia, declaring
the new tariff "null, void and no law." Effective February 1, 1833, Federal import duties would not be collected at the port of Charleston.
President Andrew Jackson responded with a threat of force. He reinforced the garrisons guarding Charleston Harbor and sent 5,000
muskets to arm his supporters in the state. Vice President Calhoun
resigned his office, to be quickly returned to Washington as senator.
If attacked, South Carolina promised to secede and fight for independence. The General Assembly passed a huge defense budget and
began to raise a 25,000-man army. Civil war seemed imminent.

Had war come in 1833, such a conflict would have pitted Carolinians against one another, as there remained a substantial unionist minority in the Palmetto State. In Charleston the dispute between unionists and advocates of states' rights spread from newspaper columns to violence on the streets of the city. Emotions ran high on both sides. The issue was not protectionism—all were opposed to that—but South Carolina's challenge to the authority of the United States. Was a man's first loyalty to his state or to the Union?[1]

William Henry Timrod was untroubled in choosing sides. One day in the midst of his work he stopped, then strode briskly from his bindery to the front of McCarter's bookstore.

"Sir I must repeat to you an ode which I have just composed, and have not yet committed [to] paper," beamed Timrod.

The eight stanzas of "Sons of the Union!" fairly shouted his national patriotism. The final two were typical.

> God! do thy high decrees
> Doom that our fathers' blood was shed in vain,
> And that our glorious Union's sacred chain
> Be snapped by Foes like these?
>
> Sons of the Union, rise!
> Stand ye not recreant by, and see
> The highest star in Freedom's galaxy
> Fling sullied from the skies!

The recitation was done "with great fervour," said the admiring McCarter. "I well remember the glowing countenance . . . and the apologies he made, when he had finished, for having troubled *me* with his effusions. He said laughingly that he had never done so before and would not do so again."[2]

Timrod may have been influenced and encouraged in his political views by his literary friend James Louis Petigru, a lawyer and the most prominent and consistent unionist in the city. Timrod, Petigru, and diplomat Joel Poinsett served together on a committee to elect unionist candidates to municipal office. Another member of Timrod's literary circle, young William Gilmore Simms, promoted Federal authority as editor of his *City Gazette*.

Capitol Hill compromise would soon defuse the issue. Senator Henry Clay of Kentucky worked out an acceptable new tariff, one much lower, and South Carolina rescinded its nullification. But many recognized that nothing had been truly settled. The principle of protectionism remained. Most importantly, the underlying issue was unresolved.[3] Did sovereignty—ultimate political power—reside in the people of the United States or in the people of the individual states? The question would continue to plague Americans of Henry Timrod's generation until it brought them to the battlefields of 1861.

During the Nullification crisis and its immediate aftermath the political establishment of South Carolina attempted to ensure loyalty by requiring officials and members of the militia to swear "true" allegiance to the state. Unionists suspected that "true" meant "supreme," and balked. William Henry Timrod fumed that the nullifiers had "abrogated to themselves a power over the consciences of men, which can be exercised only by the being who created them." The German Fusileers elected Timrod their captain, and then passed a resolution declaring that they would disband rather than take the oath.[4] It never came to that. South Carolina's unionist minority would gradually be won over in the years following Nullification. In coming decades Carolinians might disagree about the wisdom of secession, but not about the right of their state to freely leave a union it had voluntarily entered.

William Henry Timrod was by now in his forties, commander of a proud militia company, member of the German Friendly Society, a respected and well-connected citizen. Only in his religious faith did Timrod seem unsure, as he tried one church after another, often neglecting Sabbath worship altogether.[5] He continued to labor as bookbinder, though Timrod moved his business and family from their cramped quarters above McCarter's shop about 1835. Their new home would be on East Bay Street, near the Cooper River docks. Still the center of Charleston's *literati*, Timrod turned his interest to drama. He authored at least two plays, both with historical settings. Scenes from them were published in literary journals during the mid-1830s, though apparently neither was ever staged.[6]

Timrod and his friends once staged a practical joke on author and editor William Gilmore Simms. Simms was part of Timrod's circle and a fellow unionist, but perhaps took himself a little too seriously.

"There was a very simple minded youth from New Jersey, named Jacob Space, who used to frequent Timrod's shop," remembered

McCarter. "Space affected literature and especially poetry, and was a great admirer of Mr. Simms.

"One day Mr. Timrod told Space that Mr. Simms had just published a new edition of Jack the Giant Killer with notes and annotations, and suggested that he (Space) should ask him for a copy.

"I well remember the rueful countenance of poor Jacob, when after his encounter with Mr. Simms, he related to Timrod, and such members of his club as were present the furious wrath of the poet who at once saw that he was being laughed at.

"Timrod was literally convulsed with laughter in which his audience joined in most heartily.

"I don't think Mr. Simms ever forgave this affront. As for Space, he never dared go near him again."

Simms recovered in time, confessing that he was in those days often "rash & hasty, frequently violent and unjust." Years later he described William Henry Timrod as "a strong man, of quick intellect, at once sparkling and sensitive."[7]

Captain Timrod and his Fusileers would have the opportunity to win applause in one real-life drama. In early 1836 sixteen plantations on the east coast of the Territory of Florida were attacked and burned by Seminole Indians. Captured Americans were tortured and murdered. Jacksonville asked for help. St. Augustine, already crowded with refugees, was near panic as there were but a handful of local militiamen to defend the town. Volunteers from nearby states answered the call. Timrod's German Fusileers arrived in St. Augustine in September. "The citizens were overjoyed at our arrival," said the captain, "in proportion to the extreme state of terror from which we relieved them." The Charlestonians saw no combat and were back home within five months, replaced by U. S. Army troops under General Winfield Scott. "Those patriotic volunteers of South Carolina [and other states]," wrote Scott, "were, no doubt, many of them, sometimes, inefficient, from the mere awkwardness of the inexperienced; but they very generally brought with them to the war high chivalry . . ."[8]

Upon his return to Charleston Timrod soon began to suffer from ill health. Forced to resign his commission, he was employed for a time at the U. S. Custom House. The family would later assume that he contracted a fever during the expedition. Some have speculated that he already had tuberculosis or another disease that was aggravated by the Florida foray. Timrod died on July 28, 1838, at the age of forty-four and was buried in the Lutheran cemetery. Cause of death, according to the Charleston Health Office, was "debility."[9]

Henry was nine years old when his father died. His widowed mother was in middle age. Rebecca, Henry's crippled older sister, was fifteen. Emily was about eight and Edith five. A father with such literary pursuits and attainments surely influenced the boy. And Captain Timrod's reputation as a soldier was a source of pride. Still, little is known of Henry's early childhood.

It might have seemed logical for the boy to begin his education at the academy operated by the German Friendly Society, but evidence of this is lacking. That institution years earlier had been a thriving school with a good library and even a clockwork-operated planetarium.[10] Paul Hamilton Hayne first met Timrod in the seat next to his at the academy operated in Charleston by Christopher Cotes.

Cotes, a former British Army functionary, opened his school about 1820. He gained a good reputation and soon enrolled over 100 scholars. It was said that Cotes catered primarily to the "socially and financially prominent," and the widowed Thyrza Timrod must have struggled to pay the annual tuition of $100. Cotes and two assistants made up the faculty. Students in the primary grades mastered spelling, composition, arithmetic, and geography. Good handwriting was emphasized. French was taught. As they advanced, boys were introduced to the classics, algebra, history, and natural philosophy. They were expected to give orations in Latin. Cotes even bought a large telescope in England and taught astronomy. Any student unable to perform academically was quickly identified and encouraged to leave, as Cotes' goal was to prepare his young men for admission to college. Discipline was strict. Cotes "reserved the chastening of the boys exclusively for himself," remembered one who knew him. By the time students reached the age of thirteen or fourteen corporal punishment ceased, though expulsion remained an option. One morning in class Henry proudly showed Paul a poem he had just finished, "his earliest consecutive attempt at verse-making," according to Hayne. "It was a ballad of stirring adventures, and sanguinary catastrophe! But I thought it perfect— wonderful—and so, naturally, did he." Seeing the two boys together talking, Principal Cotes "meanly assaulted us in the rear, effectually quenching for the time all æsthetic enthusiasm." The schoolmaster, concluded Hayne, "united the morals of Pecksniff with the learning of Squeers."

William J. Rivers, another of Timrod's teachers, later described him as "modest and diffident, with a nervous utterance, but with melody ever in his heart and on his lips. Though always slow of speech, he was yet, like Burns, quick to learn. The chariot wheels might jar in the gates through which he tried to drive his winged steeds, but the horses were of celestial temper, and the car of purest gold."

"Shy, but neither melancholy nor morose, he was passionate, impulsive, eagerly ambitious, with a thirst for knowledge hard to satiate," wrote Paul Hayne of his friend. "But too close a devotion to books did not destroy the natural lightness and simplicity of youth. He mingled freely with his comrades, all of whom respected, while some dearly loved him. At that time he was physically active and vigorous, and delighted in every sort of rough and out-door sport; in leaping, running, wrestling, swimming, and even in *fighting.*"

Another friend remembered Henry Timrod's love of nature, that passion he shared with his mother. "How unspeakably Timrod rejoiced in the weekly holiday, with its long rambles through the field and wood! . . . . Born in a city, pent up in its dusty avenues, he longed for the untrammeled freedom of the country. He doted upon its waving fields, its deep blue skies, and the glory of the changing seasons. These formed his special delight, because in them he instinctively recognized his best teachers. Face to face with Nature he had no fears, no misgivings . . ."[11]

The earliest known Timrod poem, the playful "In Bowers of Ease," he composed when fifteen years old. During his teen years in Charleston Timrod wrote over 60 poems. A few penned at that time the public would read later. His first work to appear in print was published in the *Charleston Evening News* on September 8, 1846, signed "T. H." Timrod had written the sonnet about two years earlier, at the age of sixteen.

How Many Yearn to Tear Aside the Veil

How many yearn to tear aside the veil
    That kindly overshades Futurity,
The hidden sea on which our barks must sail
    With breezes fair or foul as it may be,

To gain or lose the port, who can foresee?—
    A fool's desire, there may be much to dread
Beyond that veil, and wouldst thou have it known
    That all thy hopes may soon be overthrown?
Blue skies above me, but a mist ahead,
    I care not wish not that it should be rent,
The moveless calm at present 'round me spread
    A courage to my timid heart has lent,
And I will onward steer with fearless soul
Though storms divide me from the long'd for goal.[12]

3

"Harry, you are a fool!"

HENRY TIMROD WAS WELL PREPARED FOR THE CLASSICAL CURRICULUM that dominated antebellum Southern higher education. He had only to choose the institution. Friends encouraged him to attend the University of Georgia, and he took their advice. The decision was a little surprising. The College of Charleston had made tremendous strides academically in the 1840s. South Carolina College in Columbia might also have been a logical choice. Under its president William Campbell Preston the school was prospering as never before.[1] But young Henry may have based his decision on the independence and adventure he envisioned in living for the first time far from home.

Tuition, board, and other expenses at the University of Georgia totaled at least $140 per year. Thyrza Timrod saw genius in her son and wanted to give him every advantage, but the cost was probably beyond her means. Fortunately, it seems that a Charleston businessman named Ross also recognized promise in the young man and was willing to help financially. The school year at Georgia began in August and was divided into three terms, each four months long. Henry was admitted as a sophomore in 1844—a member of the class scheduled to graduate in 1847—but for some reason did not enter school until the beginning of the second term. Because he began his studies on January 16, 1845, he was listed as an "irregular student."[2]

Henry boarded a passenger car at the rail depot in Charleston. The sixteen year old would travel through Branchville and Hamburg in South Carolina, then from Augusta to Athens on the Georgia Railroad. Through the windows he could see pine forests and vast plantations. Cotton fields lay fallow in the cold January sun. Smoke curled from the chimneys of mansions, slaves' quarters, and humble cabins. It would take many hours to complete the nearly 250-mile journey. Finally stepping onto the station platform in Athens, he excitedly gathered his luggage and made his way down Carr's Hill, crossed the Oconee River by ferry, then climbed another rise to the campus.

Chartered in 1795, the University of Georgia first opened its doors to students in 1801. Several handsome structures had been erected, the main building named Franklin College. The campus was noted for its two-and-one-half-acre botanical garden containing a green house and an astonishing variety of ornamental plants and fruit trees. In 1845 most of the school's 106 young men lived in dormitories, and Henry was assigned to room 31 in New College. Georgia was home of the majority of students, but three other states were represented. Seven boys were from Charleston. Unmarried professors lived in the dormitories, quartered there to preserve order and enforce the rules. Maintaining discipline was a constant struggle. College president Alonzo A. Church, a Vermont-born Presbyterian minister, had a reputation for strictness.

Church tried to leave his students with little free time, but they were not without a social life. Athens had a population of around 3,000 and was home to three female academies. There was one weekly newspaper and even a bookstore.[3] Two campus literary societies—the Demosthenian and the Phi Kappa—kept students occupied. Their members staged debates on current topics: dueling, capital punishment, women's suffrage, slavery, and Southern rights. Henry joined the Demosthenians and would soon be elected "doorkeeper." Meetings were held on Saturdays and often lasted all day. A member of the senior class made an oration before them on Independence Day, 1845. At a joint meeting of both societies in 1846, the prominent Charleston attorney James Louis Petigru spoke on "the progress of knowledge." The societies had their own meeting halls and libraries containing thousands of donated volumes. Biographies of famous men, Scott's novels, and books of poetry were the most popular.[4]

Students began each morning at 6:30 with a compulsory chapel service. Henry and the sophomore class commenced the second session of the year by delving into Horace's *Satires*, *Epistles*, and *Art of Poetry*, Sophocles' dramas, the geometry of Euclid, history, and French.

The year concluded with a study of Juvenal, the Roman poet, the Athenian tragedian Euripides, advanced geometry, logarithms, plane trigonometry, and botany. As juniors they would go on to a variety of scientific disciplines, more advanced geometry, as well as Homer's *Iliad* and Cicero's *De oratore*. According to Paul Hayne, Henry thrived on the classics. Sophocles, "sad Electra's poet," Horace, and Catullus were among his favorites. He read widely too in English poetry and literature.

"A large part of my leisure at college," Henry laughingly admitted to Paul Hayne, "was occupied in the composition of love verses, frantic or tender. Every pretty girl's face I met acted upon me like an inspiration! I fancied myself a sublimated Turk (when these faces were reproduced in day-dreams) though walking an ideal, and therefore innocent, Harem of young Beauties."[5]

In November of 1845 Henry, now almost seventeen, wrote a five-stanza poem entitled "To Love." The third stanza well summarizes his newfound theme:

> I can admire fair Nature's sheen,
>   And where a violet has been,
> Or rosebud throws its spells around
>   I deem the spot is holy ground.
> But when I meet an eye of blue,
>   It seems to me of richer hue
> Than ever deck'd the little flower
>   Of modesty in summer hour,
> And the proud rosebud's deep'ning flush
>   Is nothing to a maiden's blush.
> All other themes will I disown
>   My strains, sweet love, are thine alone.[6]

In his "Choice in Eyes," written two months later, the fickle adolescent playfully confesses to his flirtations.

> For me whatever be the dye,
> The blue the black the hazel eye,
> If it on me sweetly *smile*
> 'Tis my favourite—*for a while*.
> When it frowns I break the spell
> Another'll suit me quite as well.[7]

Marie, Isabel, Rose, Chloe, and Genevieve are among the names gleaned from verses written during his months in Athens. Two poems were penned for Anne Waddel. One was an acrostic: the beginning letter of each of its ten lines spelled her name. Anne was the daughter of James P. Waddel, the university's professor of ancient languages.[8] The six lines of "Written in a Psalm Book" tell much about the young poet's feelings at seventeen:

> What! must I not confide in men?
> I'll ope my heart to *woman* then,
> Make her the guide-star of life,
> On her my every hope I'll fling,
> To her in trust forever cling
> For solace in this world of strife.[9]

With such diversions, Henry seemed to have trouble keeping his mind on school work and responsibilities. In his own handwriting, and a friend's, are preserved a series of notes passed back and forth—presumably in class—as they gossiped about the engagement of a "Miss S." In June of 1845 Henry was charged by fellow Demosthenians "for having absented himself from the society for three consecutive meetings." On this occasion he was able to conjure up a satisfactory excuse. It would be remembered by some townsfolk that Timrod "spent a rather shiftless life" in Athens, and while at the university "his habits were bad."[10] The institution itself was known as "a rich man's school," where serious scholars were all too rare. Of those who entered the university during the antebellum years, a full forty percent left without graduating. Many were expelled for such offenses as "disorderly conduct," "disrespect to professors," fighting, and even assault. The common denominator was often alcohol, and drinking may have been one of Henry Timrod's weaknesses as well.[11]

"He was a peculiar and in many ways a most charming and delightful character," wrote one who knew him. "Reserved around strangers, yet eager for appreciation and recognition, high strung and easily offended even by the friends he loved passionately, sometimes extremely melancholy yet full of droll humor, extravagant when he had the money to be, an excessive drinker at times, sometimes guilty of association with comrades of unapproved morals; yet all these seem to be secondary to his pure aspirations, his love for home and peace, and his religious yearnings and unfaltering trust."[12]

It was assumed by Hayne that Timrod's college career was cut short because of financial problems or ill health. Nothing in the records indicates that he failed academically, was disciplined, or was expelled. The university's tuition book shows four payments, from January 1845 to January 1846, totaling $102.23. This would have covered tuition for two years, though not, of course, other necessary expenses. The last record of Timrod in connection with the University of Georgia is a mention by the Demosthenian Society on March 14, 1846. Sometime later that year he left, at least twelve months short of graduation.[13]

"And now the battle of existence opened in grim earnest," wrote Paul Hayne of his eighteen year old friend. "Timrod's first move upon returning to his native city, was to enter, as a student, the office of that distinguished lawyer, James L. Petigru, Esq."[14] As far as we know Timrod had never expressed any interest in the law, but may have undertaken the training to please his mother. Since there was no law school in South Carolina, those wanting to become lawyers would study under the direction of a practicing attorney. Petigru permitted a number of young men to "read the law" under his supervision. A few steps from the courthouse, in the shadow of St. Michael's Church, Petigru had just built a handsome new office for his thriving practice. Timrod minimized expenses by staying at home with his mother, sister Rebecca, and seventy-three year old grandmother Sarah Prince. Any income he earned must have been meager. The young man's poetic output fell off sharply as he set to work to become a lawyer.

Still, Timrod found what time he could for literature and congenial company. He would join others his age for conversation, debate, and dramatic readings at the Mechanic's Library Association. His friend John Dickson Bruns described him around this time as having a "square jaw," with "gray eyes set deep under heavy brows." "Timrod was fond of argument," remembered Hayne, "but as extemporaneous speaker, he had not . . . inherited his father's facility of language and illustration." Yet he was, added Hayne, "an admirable reader, even if his style *did* sometimes verge upon the theatrical." Short in stature, with a bass voice, "his superb head well set upon shoulders erect, and thrown back in haughty grace—his gray eyes flashing, and his swarthy face one glow of intense emotion—it was impossible to listen to him without catching some spark of his fiery enthusiasm." In reciting poetry another remembered Timrod "giving such expression and pathos to lines that many would gloss over and forget."[15]

Soon Timrod and his friends were among those meeting at the spacious new bookstore on King Street, between Hasell and Wentworth, opened by John Russell. This "literary emporium," said Hayne, "became in time the *rendezvous* of all the *savants*, the professionals, and the *literati* of the city." In the rear of the store, behind bookshelves and counters, was an area lit by gaslight and heated with a coal-burning stove. There, seated on chairs and sofas, men met to discuss the latest books, tell stories, and argue the issues of the day. Petigru continued to represent the older generation. Timrod and Hayne were regulars, as was the young classicist Basil Gildersleeve. Patrick Lynch, Catholic priest and master of ancient Greek, joined the group. Others of the informal club included James W. Miles and his brother William Porcher Miles, William J. Grayson, David Ramsey, and Latin scholar John della Torre. John R. Thompson, editor of the *Southern Literary Messenger,* visited from Virginia in the spring of 1849. Russell's soon became the focus of Charleston's intellectual life, even as the city itself was arguably the center of Southern culture. "Those who could not travel were intense Charlestonians," remembered Gildersleeve, "and those who could were not much less intense. Men who knew both Paris and Charleston spoke respectfully of Charleston."[16]

Timrod was once the victim of a practical joke contrived by his literary cohorts. John della Torre translated a recently published Timrod poem into "elegant Latin," then wrote the lines inside a volume of medieval verse. When Timrod and friends assembled, della Torre produced the book and read the poem aloud as if he had discovered it in the thirteenth-century collection.

John Dickson Bruns turned sternly to Timrod and accused him of having "put our friendship to the severest test" by his plagiarism.

"Bruns," replied Timrod, "I assure you on my honor I have never before heard or read a line of the verses found by della Torre. I am astonished by the extraordinary similarity of the poems, and it would seem to prove what I have long wildly dreamed, that there is truth in metempsychosis, and that in some previous state of existence I was the Latin poet himself."

His friends kept straight faces as long as they could, then—with a sigh of relief from Timrod—let him in on their prank.[17]

A number of Timrod poems appeared in the Charleston press. "They became, *locally*, quite popular," wrote Hayne, "and, in one instance, to the author's intense delight, his verses were set to music." Soon after Thompson's visit, Timrod's work began to be published in the *Southern Literary Messenger*. He chose to sign them "Aglaus," the name of a virtually unknown ancient Greek pastoral poet.[18] "Sonnet: Poet! If on a Lasting Fame" appeared in Thompson's journal only two months after the editor's return to Richmond.[19] Over the next year eight more Timrod poems found a place in the *Messenger*. Most were love poems. Some began to show a growing maturity of theme and expression. In the first stanza of "Vox et Praeterea Nihil" (a voice and thereafter nothing) he seemed to confirm his call to poetry.

> I'VE been haunted all night, I've been haunted all day,
> By the ghost of a song, by the shade of a lay,
> That with meaningless words and profusion of rhyme,
> To a dreamy and musical rhythm keeps time.
> A simple, but still a most magical strain,
> Its dim monotones have bewildered my brain
> With a specious and cunning appearance of thought,
> I seem to be catching but never have caught.[20]

In December of 1850 Timrod celebrated his twenty-second birthday, but by then he had abandoned the study of law. It was a pursuit he found "distasteful," though he had kept at it for some time. He thought of entering the teaching profession at the college level, but was unable to find employment. As a non-graduate, the most he could have hoped for would have been a position as college instructor or tutor. But poetry paid few bills. He had to find a way to make a living.

An episode during his final days in Petigru's office epitomized Timrod's dilemma.

"Timrod was too wholly a poet to keep company long with so relentless, rugged, and exacting a mistress as the law!" remembered George S. Bryan, a lawyer friend of Timrod's. "As a curious illustration of the abstraction and reverie which so often absorbed the poet, he told me that Mr. Petigru sent him on *one* occasion to take a message to a certain Factor on the Bay. But as ill luck would have it, when he had gone half way he found he had forgotten, if indeed he ever really knew, the message entrusted to his care. What was to be done? He could only return, and, with as bold a face as possible, acknowledged his misfortune.

"On his doing so, Mr. Petigru saluted him, very much excited, in his highest squeaking voice, *Why Harry, you are a fool!*' And, added our poet friend to me, 'I would have been a fool to Mr. Petigru to the end of my days, even if I revealed in afterlife the genius of a Milton or a Shakespeare.'"[21]

4

"Praeceptor Amat"

Tᴉᴍʀᴏᴅ ᴄʜᴏsᴇ ᴛᴏ ʙᴇᴄᴏᴍᴇ ᴀ ᴛᴇᴀᴄʜᴇʀ, ᴛᴜᴛᴏʀɪɴɢ ᴄʜɪʟᴅʀᴇɴ ᴏғ plantation families. His first position, beginning probably in the fall of 1850, was regrettable and brief. Timrod's employer was Charles Lowndes, a Low-Country planter who lived not far from Charleston. The story is told of Timrod returning to the city after having been paid $300, perhaps half his annual salary. A day later Lowndes ran into his tutor on a city street. Timrod was distraught. "Like a fool, I have squandered my last dollar," he moaned, "damn my idiotic soul! literally thrown it away, damn my idiotic soul!"[1]

Things could only get better. By early 1851, Timrod had found employment with Daniel Blake. The forty-nine year old Blake, born in England, had made his fortune producing cotton. Owner of "Combahee" plantation in St. Bartholomew's Parish, Colleton District, South Carolina, he and his family spent their summers in Buncombe County, North Carolina. Emily Blake, thirteen years her husband's junior, was the mother of six children. Four were of school age and became Timrod's charges: Frederick, 13; Daniel, 10; Fanny, 9; and Henry, 8. It was his duty to provide a primary education for the younger children and to give the boys the grounding they would need later for college.

Their North Carolina mountain home, "The Meadows," was on Cane Creek, a tributary of the French Broad River, in a locality famous for the Catawba grape. Timrod was delighted with his first Appalachian summer. In a letter to his sister in Charleston he reported high temperature readings in June of but seventy-two degrees. "This is better than King St.—isn't it?" He praised too the Blake estate and its mountainous surroundings. "The house stands on an eminence which was once a rough and broken hill, but which has been for the most part leveled for the purpose of making a fine, spacious garden. This garden is laid out much in the English fashion, with graveled walks and plots of green turf—in the midst of which are set flowers of many varieties. I have never seen more beautiful roses than one can pick here 'ad libitum.' To the north, the garden descends first by a double terrace and then by a smooth but precipitous slope to a miniature valley through which prattles a very pretty little brook. Thence the ground rises again by a gradual ascent, and on this side is the fruit and vegetable garden. Beyond this, and also to the east from the flower garden you see fields of waving grain and meadows of the brightest verdure, and skirting these, the woods commence and run up to the very summits of the mountains that form the background of the landscape."

Timrod expressed satisfaction with his teaching duties, adding that "Mr. and Mrs. Blake profess to be much pleased with me." Emily Blake was "a good French scholar herself," said Timrod, and thought his pronunciation "elegant." His only complaint was "a dearth of news and gossip in this part of the country." He wrote on Independence Day, perhaps the quietest one he had experienced. "How are you spending the Fourth in Charleston—here Heaven knows it is dull enough."[2]

Recipient of Timrod's letter was his twenty-four-year-old sister Emily. Her husband, George Munro Goodwin, was a native of England, where his father and nine-year-old sister Kate still lived. There were two young children in George and Emily Goodwin's home. Edith W. Goodwin may have been named for her Aunt Edith. Four-year-old Catherine (called Katie) was probably given the name of her father's English sister. The Goodwin family had only recently resided in Darlington District where George worked as a clerk in a country store owned by Colonel William Henry Cannon, a wealthy planter and merchant active in politics and the militia.[3]

In October of 1851 Timrod was still at the Blakes' mountain home when he beheld an aurora borealis, a rare display of nature that he admittedly did not understand scientifically. "The show commenced about an hour after sunset," he wrote Emily, "with a beautiful rose colour towards the Northeast which slowly diffused itself over the whole Northern heavens. While this was going on a light appeared on the Northern horizon just as if morning were breaking in that direction. Gradually this light took the form of a pale green cloud shaping itself like a segment of a circle. . . . The rose colour had died away, when the segment began to emit streams of light—at first of the same colour as itself, then changing to rose colour and again becoming pale green. So it kept on fading and brightening until twelve o'clock. It was the most astonishing and beautiful spectacle I have ever seen."

He could have written "a dozen papers" describing the lights, Timrod told his sister. Emily had already declared his letters the best she received. "Heaven help your correspondents then," he replied. "They must be miserable things. There are no letters with which I take so little pains as those I write home."[4] He and Emily shared an interest in literature. On one occasion he remarked on Charlotte Brontë's just-published novel *Villette*, finding it inferior to *Jane Eyre*. "It is by no means a bread and butter thing however," and he praised the author's "skill in sky and weather painting."[5]

By mid-November he hoped to visit the Goodwins in Charleston, but feared that Daniel Blake would want him to accompany the family to their Colleton District, South Carolina, home. Timrod did not want to refuse. "Yet I am half mad when I think of spending another winter on a low country plantation," he concluded, perhaps remembering his former position with Lowndes.[6]

Rural isolation deprived him of the social and intellectual stimulation of the city—as well as its temptations—but did allow Timrod ample time for reading and contemplation. Months spent at "Combahee" and "The Meadows" encouraged his writing of nature poetry. The sonnet "Fate! Seek Me Out Some Lake" appeared in the *Southern Literary Messenger* that first July with the Blakes. He imagines himself peacefully adrift upon the still waters of a mountain lake,

> Shut in by wooded hills that steeply rise,
> And beautiful with blue inverted skies,—[7]

The poet seeks rest and relief from his discontent in "The Summer Bower," and there finds Nature willing

> To sympathize with human suffering;
> But for the pains, the fever, and the fret
> Engendered of a weak, unquiet heart,

She hath no solace; and who seeks her when
These be the troubles over which he moans,
Reads in her unreplying lineaments
Rebukes, that, to the guilty consciousness,
Strike like contempt.[8]

In the sonnet "I Scarcely Grieve" he concludes that even though city born

Here, too, O Nature! in this haunt of Art,
Thy power is on me, and I own thy thrall.[9]

Timrod would return to Charleston, his "haunt of Art," as often as teaching duties permitted, usually during spring and winter holidays. He enjoyed these reunions with family and friends. William Gilmore Simms, now in middle age, had already published dozens of novels, histories, and volumes of verse. Simms "delighted to gather round him the younger literary men of his acquaintance," remembered Paul Hayne, "and to discuss with them the thousand and one topics connected with art and letters." Timrod's boyhood friend Hayne had graduated from the College of Charleston, studied law under Petigru, and been admitted to the South Carolina bar. An early convert to secessionism, Hayne expressed his political views in the newspaper *Palmetto Flag*. He married in 1852, that year joining the *Southern Literary Gazette* as associate editor. Hayne soon journeyed to Boston in search of a publisher for his poetry. While there he met Henry Wadsworth Longfellow, Ralph Waldo Emerson, and Oliver Wendell Holmes.[10] As Hayne's career seemed to be soaring, it would have been natural for Timrod to feel left behind, teaching children in the country, contributing poems to journals that paid little, and virtually unknown outside of his own circle.

Those who knew him remembered that Timrod "never wore his heart upon his sleeve, was reserved in his manner to the general public . . . but with his intimate friends he would utterly unbend." Hayne recalled "little suppers" at Simms' Charleston home, with "none of the guests, perhaps, enjoying themselves as vividly as Timrod, whose excitable temperament, and keenly social proclivities, made his whole heart expand in the companionship of those he loved and trusted." Another favorite meeting place was a tavern on the east side of lower King Street operated by a free black man, Nat

Fuller. It was said that Timrod often drank too much, and afterwards felt profound shame over his intemperance.

Described by one as short, with regular features and small hands and feet, Timrod "dressed habitually in a neat black suit, but was often compelled to wear his clothes, especially his shoes, until they were in need of repair." A pale complexion contrasted with dark brown hair and mustache. Eyes, "though slightly melancholy in repose flashed with excitement and sparkled with mirth under their long curling lashes. His voice was deep rich bass, very soft and musical." Those eyes were of little use to him once the sun set. "He was afflicted with nightblindness and had to be piloted around after dark."[11]

Timrod remained with the Blakes for about three years, teaching the children and observing the older generation as well. He came to a few unorthodox conclusions. In "Dramatic Fragment," published in the *Southern Literary Gazette* on Christmas Day, 1852, he decried the conventional wisdom that children must be made to conform.

> We treat these little ones too much like flowers,
> Training them, in blind selfishness, to deck
> Sticks of our poor setting, when they might,
> If left to clamber where themselves incline
> Find nobler props to cling to, fitter place,
> And sweeter air to bloom in.

Timrod saw the journey from youth to maturity as growth, to be sure, but not change.

> Yes! what is childhood
> But after all a sort of golden daylight,
> A beautiful and blessed wealth of sunshine,
> Wherein the powers and passions of the soul
> Sleep starlike but existent, till the night
> Of gathering years shall call the slumberers forth,
> And they rise up in glory? Early grief,
> A shadow like the darkness of eclipse,
> Hath sometimes waked them sooner.[12]

Soul-deadening materialism was the bane he condemned in "Youth and Manhood." Timrod scorned to take the "wide and winding road" leading downward,

> Where manhood plays;
>
> Plays with the baubles and the gauds of earth—
>   Wealth, power, and fame—
> Nor knows that in the twelvemonth after birth
>   He did the same.
>
> Where the descent begins, through long defiles
>   I see them wind;
> And some are looking down with hopeful smiles,
>   And some are—blind.

Rather than join the lifeless throng of Philistines who "toil and plod," he prays God would first

> Give me to chant one pure and deathless lay;
>   And let me die![13]

Timrod may have spent most of 1854 as a tutor with the extended Palmer family of Santee, South Carolina, although records are few.[14] Paul Hayne described Timrod in May of that year in a letter to a friend. "He is a man of true genius (I use the word in its high, & legitimate signification—) of the noblest disposition, and the most sincere affections." Hayne confided that Longfellow had praised Timrod's work. Unfortunately, Timrod's "situation in society is not agreeable. He is poor, & humbly born, & of course, with his temperament—proud, & will make advances to no one—But let him once experience kindness, & his heart becomes open as the day." Hayne recommended that his friend, a woman with literary interests, write to Timrod. "If *you begin* a correspondence with him, he will be your friend for life—Besides you will be securing to yourself the friendship of a Poet, whose name will stand higher yet."[15]

Sometime before April of 1856 Timrod was working in Orangeburg District, having accepted a tutoring position in the home of Murray Robinson. Robinson was thirty-nine. His wife Felicia, thirty-three, was born in Bordeaux, France. There were five school-age children in the family: Jude, 16; Murray, Jr., 14; Kirk, 13; John, 11; and Felicia, 8. Rails had been laid through the district more than a decade earlier. About eight miles south of the courthouse town of Orangeburg the railroad erected a woodshed, water tank, and pump at a settlement that came to be known as Rowe's Pump. Murray Robinson bought a plantation near there called "Oak Grove," and moved his family from Charleston.[16]

Orangeburg District lay between Charleston and the state capital of Columbia. The census of 1850 revealed that two-thirds of the district's 23,582 people were slaves, and that half of all households held slaves. The Robinsons grew cotton with a work force of 69 bondsmen.[17] All depended on cotton, the district's only cash crop, for their livelihood, and the institution of slavery was unquestioned. Southerners knew that slavery had existed since antiquity, was sanctioned by the Bible, and had supported American economic life since colonial times. The rise of antislavery sentiment in the North—and calls for slavery's violent overthrow—gave cause for alarm. In April 1856 the *Southron*, Orangeburg's newspaper, printed a speech by local congressman Lawrence Massillon Keitt denouncing "aggressions upon the South" perpetrated by Abolitionists. As if to back up his words, the same issue announced a parade of the militia's 14th Infantry Regiment, that order signed by their colonel, Paul A. Mc-Michael.[18]

The conflict seemed distant to Timrod. In February 1856 he had for the first time published a poem in the *Southern Literary Messenger* over his own name, and was surprised to receive a letter asking for his autograph. For three years he had published relatively little, but at the Robinsons' his output became prolific. "These woods and grounds seem to help me to think," he said.[19] During one two-week period he reported "having written oceans of rhyme." And now there was a journal in Timrod's native city eager to publish his work. "A few of the scholars and cultivated gentlemen of Charleston conceived the notion," wrote Hayne, "of establishing a monthly literary magazine in that city. It was designed to be a representative organ, not merely of local, but of *Southern* intellect, taste, and opinions." Bookstore proprietor John Russell became publisher and business manager. Hayne agreed to take on the task of editor. For $3 per year subscribers were promised to be kept abreast of "the progress of a sound American literature, free from party shackles or individual prejudice." On April 1, 1857, the first number of *Russell's Magazine* went out.[20]

"The Arctic Voyager," Timrod's initial contribution to *Russell's*, was published in the premiere edition. Fascinated by reports of arctic exploration, imagery of "the ice-bound world" would become a recurring theme of his. In 1845 two British ships under the command of John Franklin disappeared while looking for the Northwest Passage, that illusory route from the Atlantic to the Pacific. A number of rescue missions were attempted. One American-financed effort set out in the summer of 1850, but failed to find Franklin. The surgeon on that expedition, Elisha Kent Kane, made another try two years later with his own ship. Trapped in the ice for two years, Kane and his men experienced terrible hardship before being rescued. They never located Franklin or discovered an open polar sea, but did much exploring. Before he died in 1856, at the age of thirty-seven, Kane published a two-volume account of his quest. The best seller was illustrated with 300 woodcuts and twenty-one engravings made from his own sketches. "Midnight in September" had the sun hanging on a frozen horizon. There were pictures of weird rock formations and titanic icebergs that dwarfed Kane's vessel.[21] Readers like Timrod were introduced to a harshly beautiful world they could hardly have imagined. Kane himself is the narrator of Timrod's poem, the hero who kept struggling northward

> Till I had seen the star which never sets
> Freeze in the Arctic zenith.

Though Kane met defeat, he was steadfast in his faith that

> A lofty hope, if earnestly pursued,
> Is its own crown, and never in this life
> Is labour wholly fruitless.[22]

On May Day, 1857, Timrod attended a *tableau vivant* staged by schoolgirls in the town of Orangeburg. One scene depicted a bride on her wedding day, calling forth the flood of emotions felt by the girl's mother. That poem—"Stanzas"—appeared in *Russell's*.[23] During these months he wrote a number of love poems, at least one for his latest interest—a Charleston girl named Julia. "I do not wish she should be aware," he wrote to a confidant, "how much of my heart (a big one you know) she holds in her hands. But you must not let her forget me for all that."[24] "Retirement" was published by *Russell's* in July. In it he rejects the common notion that men are born "for bat-

tle only." A better wisdom is found in calm contemplation around
the hearth at home. The poet advises building

> A wall of quiet thought, and gentle books,
> Betwixt us and the hard and bitter world.

Timrod published no fewer than four poems in the July issue of *Russell's*. The longest, "A Rhapsody of a Southern Winter Night," might
be compared to "The Summer Bower," except that languor has
given way to a glad and hopeful heart. He described how a smiling,
frolicking child climbed a fence to pick a flower, and "laughed my
gloom away."[25]

That child was probably Felicia Robinson, now ten years old, his
favorite pupil. In the fall of 1857 he wrote about his relationship
with her in a poem he initially called "The Tutor." It would appear in
Russell's as "Praeceptor Amat" (the tutor loves). He playfully confessed affection for this "child of the weather," a charmer who would
rather gather flowers than study her lessons. Timrod's fondness for
Felicia forced him to feign indifference lest he reveal his feelings.
His sentimental fancy, however innocent, resonated romantic love.
While "sick of the mask I must wear," he is yet scrupulous to remain
"the stern, passionless Tutor." He delayed publication of the poem
for several months, perhaps until he could feel sure that his words
would not be misunderstood.[26]

Timrod spent about two years with the Robinson family, seemingly the happiest of his tutorial career. Even after he left their employ he would often visit them when passing through Orangeburg
District by rail. "I remember Mr. Timrod well," wrote Felicia Robinson Chisolm decades later. "With us he was like a member of our
family, making himself such by his unobtrusive, gentle nature, and
by the deep interest which he always took in our affairs. He was very
considerate, sympathetic and affectionate in disposition. I have
heard him spoken of as a 'crank,' which is unjust. He was very absent-minded, and was often so absorbed in poetical fancies that he
would appear peculiar." If Timrod forgot, for example, his place in
the children's lessons or recitations he might attempt to escape his
dilemma by simply exclaiming, "Now begin!" When not teaching,
Timrod was invariably reading—often Tennyson or Wordsworth.
"He was a very learned man," concluded Felicia, "being devoted to

the classics, and able to read fluently French, German, Latin and Greek."[27]

It was probably during Timrod's final months with the Robinsons that sister Emily and her family returned to Darlington District, where George would again work for William Henry Cannon. His Charleston business had failed. It must have been a tearful time as Emily again left friends and loved ones in the city of her birth. Goodwin would serve Cannon as overseer, bookkeeper, and—perhaps with Emily's help—operate Cannon's store near the town of Florence in the Mars Bluff section. About a mile east of his own home, "Orange Grove," Cannon built a comfortable house for the Goodwins that they would call "Forest Cottage."

During a visit to the Goodwins, probably in early 1858, Timrod was hired to teach in the Cannon household. Colonel Cannon and his wife Anna had five children of school age: William H., 14; George H., 12; Robert, 11; Sarah C., 10; and Ella E., 8. It is not known which family Timrod lived with while employed as a tutor, but Cannon built a tiny schoolhouse for his use.[28]

Physician Edward Porcher was a neighbor and Timrod soon became one of his patients. It may have been Dr. Porcher who first diagnosed Timrod, now nearing thirty, as having tuberculosis. It was an all too common ailment. Known for thousands of years, consumption—as it was called—struck all classes of society. "These unfortunates," wrote one contemporary medical authority, "are instantly recognisable by their scrawny body, flat, narrow or concave chest . . . irregularly harsh instead of silky breathing and of course the high probability that they had elder tubercular kin with similar characteristics." There was a popular notion that "depravity or spiritual anguish" brought on the disease. It would be another century before the discovery that the microorganism responsible usually entered the lungs by being inhaled, or that it could be contracted simply by drinking unpasteurized milk. The bacilli might remain dormant until resistance was low. Symptoms included fatigue, weight loss, poor appetite, fever, and a persistent cough. The bacteria produced lesions in the lungs of victims. Sufferers often spat up blood, and as the disease progressed massive hemorrhages could occur. Nineteenth century remedies were as abundant as they were useless. Healers often prescribed cod-liver oil, and the bleeding of consumptive patients had not entirely gone out of fashion. Laudanum, a concoction of alcohol and opium, was popular—but probably too expensive for Timrod.

Dr. Porcher's home and office were under one roof, and on more than one occasion Mrs. Porcher, who read Timrod's poetry, invited him to stay for refreshments. The patient declined. Timrod truly appreciated their kindness and they thought him "timid." Anxious and unwell, he may simply have felt unable to socialize under the circumstances.

That same year—1858—a physician in Bury St. Edmund's, England, was prescribing a sea voyage and warmer climate for the declining health of his patient. George Marriott Goodwin took his advice, deciding to visit his son's family in America. Sixteen-year-old Kate would accompany her father on the journey. Neither had seen George in many years, and they had never met Emily and the children. Tragically, the elder Goodwin did not regain his health in South Carolina. Three months after their arrival he was dead.

The grieving young Kate had a decision to make. She could return to England to live with her stepmother, or she could remain with brother George and his family. She chose to stay. The visitor had become an immigrant. There would be enormous adjustments to make as Kate Goodwin exchanged Suffolk County in Victoria's England for antebellum South Carolina.

For a time she would join the other pupils in the little schoolhouse. Her teacher, said a Cannon daughter, "scarcely noticed her."[29]

5

"Our young Carolina Petrarch"

HENRY TIMROD WOULD PUBLISH NOT ONLY VERSE IN *RUSSELL'S*. WITH extraordinary clarity he discussed his craft in a series of essays in that magazine. He regretted that "the popular heart understands very little about poetry, and cares less." Poetry, like serious music, has a limited audience. His observations came from a lifetime of experience. The "popular heart"—impervious to poetry—Timrod regarded as not truly human at all, but "only a mean, narrow, unintelligent thing, which beats sometimes under fine broadcloth, and sometimes under coarser textures, to the tune of dollars and cents." The specific subject of this first article, in May 1857, was "The Character and Scope of the Sonnet." Fourteen lines of iambic pentameter in a set rhyme scheme were dismissed as "artificial" by some. "It *is* artificial," wrote Timrod, "but only as all forms of verse are artificial. There are persons who imagine poetry to be the result of some mystical inspiration, scarcely to be subjected to the bounds of space and time." He quoted Wordsworth's understanding of poetry as "emotion recollected in tranquility." Inspiration and composition are necessarily separated in time. Timrod found himself

> unable to see the stigma conveyed in the term artificial, as applied to the sonnet. The poet is an artist, and, we suppose, he regards every sort of stanza as but the artificial mould into which he pours his thought. The very restriction so much complained of, he knows to be, in some respects, an advantage. It forces him to condensation; and if it sometimes induces a poetaster to stretch a thought to the finest tenuity, what argument is that against the sonnet? As well might Jones object to the violin of Paganini, because his neighbor Smith is a wretched fiddler.[1]

Two months later William J. Grayson, a sixty-eight-year-old member of the partnership that launched *Russell's*, published an essay in which he attempted to define poetry. It was not the ideas or words, but "the form in which these words are arranged" that constituted poetry in Grayson's rigid, classical definition.[2] Timrod was quick to respond. His "What is Poetry?" came out in October. Poetry and prose may not be so easily distinguished, insisted Timrod: "the philosophic critic would as soon think of contrasting a virtue with a colour." Because a novel such as *Ivanhoe* is not a poem, it cannot be concluded "that it does not contain a single element of poetry." Some long poems, on the other hand, may not be entirely poetry. And the poet *must* use a different vocabulary in his work, wrote Timrod, "compelled, by his passion-fused imagination, to give it life, form, or colour. Hence the necessity of employing the sensuous, or concrete words of the language . . ."[3]

The unique and difficult challenges facing Southern writers were Timrod's subject in "Literature in the South," appearing in August 1859. His complaints were bitter. If a Southern author published a book in the North he was ignored there and criticized at home for going outside of his own section. Yet if he chose a Southern publisher, the work failed to sell. If the author portrayed Southern society in a positive way the North was abusive, the South ungrateful. If expressive of universal thoughts the South criticized it as "not sufficiently Southern in spirit," while the North dismissed it as a "specimen of Southern commonplace." Even educated Southerners Timrod thought too often "provincial" and lacking "a high critical culture." Certainly there was an abundance of material for writers in the history, society, and scenery of the South. But he reminded readers that Shakespeare could remain an Englishman while he dramatized ancient Rome. Likewise, Southern authors should not be constrained "never to pass the Potomac on one side, or the Gulf on the other . . . No! the domain of genius is as wide as the world, and as ancient as creation. Wherever the angel of its inspiration may lead, it has the right to follow . . ."

Southerners did not, in Timrod's view, sufficiently support with "patronage and applause" the literature they already possessed.

> Of all our Southern writers, not one but Poe has received his due measure of fame. The immense resources and versatile powers of Simms are to this day grudgingly acknowledged, or contemptuously

denied. There have been writers among us who, in another country, would have been complimented with repeated editions, whose names are now almost forgotten, and whose works it is now utterly impossible to obtain.

He professed to see a better day coming. There would be recognition for Southern writers "who know how to embody the spirit of their country without sinking that universality which shall commend their lessons to all mankind."[4]

"We see in the Cheraw papers," noted a Columbia magazine in May 1859, "accounts of the Lecture of Henry Timrod, our young Carolina Petrarch, who has been holding forth on 'The Southern Author.'"[5] He had probably delivered as a speech what would become the essay. Cheraw, a village less than forty miles north of Mars Bluff, might seem an unlikely venue for a literary discourse. But their guest speaker had a new confidence about him. The "Carolina Petrarch" was about to bolster his own standing as a man of letters with the publication of a volume of verse.

The collection would include some of the best poems he had written during the past decade, and a number penned for the occasion. The little volume was published by the Boston firm of Ticknor and Fields, the project subsidized by admiring friends. Titled simply *Poems*, the book had "1860" on its title page, though it was copyrighted in 1859 and appeared late that year. Sales proved to be disappointing, but the author was proud of his work. The few reviews were gratifying. Richard H. Stoddard, a New York literary critic, said he was "charmed" by the book. "In this modest volume," wrote *Harper's*, "we find the indications of true poetical genius. . . . Mr. Timrod's name now comes before us for the first time, but he has given assurance in this volume that he will not remain a stranger in the walks of American poetry." Hayne, of course, was delighted with his friend's effort. "Timrod possesses more ability, (*native*, & acquired,)—than *all* the other *young* poets of the *South*, placed together," he wrote privately. One "old" Southern poet to praise Timrod's work was William Gilmore Simms. There had been something of a falling out between the two men, each proud of his own abilities and both sharp of tongue. Simms recognized Timrod's extraordinary talent. "But, save with the friends of the author, his book may be said to have fallen dead from the press," said Simms. From experience, he thought he knew why. "Northern criticism was silent.—New England criticism is always silent in respect to the swans of other regions. Its own geese are its sufficient swans."[6]

The most ambitious work in Timrod's book was "A Vision of Poesy," a 558-line exploration of the mission of the poet and the meaning of his medium. "Poesy, the angel of the earth," visits a young poet and offers him her wisdom.

> "And ever since that immemorial hour,
>   When the glad morning-stars together sung,
> My task hath been, beneath a mightier Power,
>   To keep the world forever fresh and young;
> I give it not its fruitage and its green,
> But clothe it with a glory all unseen.
>
> . . . .
>
> "Before my power the kings of earth have bowed;
>   I am the voice of Freedom, and the sword
> Leaps from its scabbard when I call aloud;
>   Wherever life in sacrifice is poured,
> Wherever martyrs die or patriots bleed,
> I weave the chaplet and award the meed.
>
> . . . .
>
> "And he must be as armed warrior strong,
>   And he must be as gentle as a girl,
> And he must front, and sometimes suffer wrong,
>   With brow unbent, and lip untaught to curl;
> For wrath, and scorn, and pride, however just,
> Fill the clear spirit's eyes with earthly dust."[7]

In November 1859, after working on two occasions for Colonel Cannon, George Goodwin moved to Columbia to become a merchant. In a few months he would report to a census-taker that he owned personal property valued at $300, but no real estate. Besides wife Emily, also part of the Goodwin household were daughters Edith, Kate, and Anna, son Henry, and sister Kate, now eighteen. Henry Timrod made frequent trips to see them. "Dear little ones!" he wrote later of Emily's children. "What is the difference between a niece and a daughter is a mystery which I trust the next two or three years will solve for me."[8]

On one visit Timrod stopped by the campus residence of Augustus Baldwin Longstreet, president of South Carolina College. Seventy years old and nearing the end of a varied career, Longstreet and his wife were delighted to receive guests. Yale graduate, Methodist minister, legislator, and judge—he gained his greatest fame as the author of *Georgia Scenes,* a colorful recounting of life on the Southern frontier. One evening in February 1860 student Charles Hutson and a friend called on the Longstreets. "So, we sat down, and the old Judge got his pipe and fell to smoking, and we all chatted together, until the arrival of another visitor. This was Mr. Timrod, the young Charleston poet, quite a nice-looking but very little man. He behaved himself very well. During the conversation he spoke of a peculiarly sweet and plaintive Indian air, which he had heard that the Judge played, whereupon that gentleman very obligingly got up and fetched his flute (an elegant glass one) and played the air for us."[9]

Timrod may have met his latest love interest through Longstreet. The college president knew Sophia Wentz Sosnowski, headmistress of the South Carolina Female Collegiate Institute at Barhamville, on the outskirts of Columbia. Madame Sosnowski's daughter, Sophie, taught at the school. Timrod was immediately attracted to the twenty-three-year-old teacher of literature and music. Born in Pennsylvania, Sophia Augusta was the oldest child of Joseph Stanislaus Sosnowski, an exile from Poland who died when she was a child. Sophie had a sister Caroline (called Kallie) and a brother named Julius.[10]

It was said that Sophie possessed an extraordinary singing voice. She read serious books, appreciated literature, and spoke fluent German. Timrod could only be fascinated by this accomplished, intelligent young woman. Predictably, he soon found himself in love. Sophie seemingly enjoyed the attention, but would not be so easily won. She put him off, even claiming that she was determined to remain single. He took her words literally and set about, in a poem, to change her mind.

> You say, as one who shapes a life,
> That you will never be a wife,
>
> And, laughing lightly, ask my aid
> To paint your future as a maid.

In the first section of "Two Portraits" Timrod paints a picture of Sophie in middle age, having never married. The portrait is not unkind, nor is it altogether unattractive.

> Your eyes, grown deeper, are not sad,
> Yet never more than gravely glad;
>
> And the old charm still lurks within
> The cloven dimple of your chin.
>
> Some share, perhaps, of youthful gloss
> Your cheek hath shed; but still across
>
> The delicate ear are folded down
> Those silken locks of chestnut brown;
>
> Though here and there a thread of gray
> Steals through them like a lunar ray.

He concedes that she might lead a useful life. She would have the love and help of family and friends. Still, there is an unavoidable sadness.

> Ah! we would wish the world less fair,
> If spring alone adorned the year,
>
> And autumn came not with its fruit,
> And autumn hymns were ever mute.
>
> So I remark with small surprise
> That, as the unvarying season flies,
>
> From day to night and night to day,
> You sicken of your endless May.

Timrod shows Sophie a better way, in the satisfaction she might enjoy as wife and mother.

> An air of still, though bright repose
> Tells that a tender hand bestows
>
> All that a generous manhood may

To make your life one bridal day,
. . . .

Your voice was always soft in youth,
And had the very sound of truth,

But never were its tones so mild
Until you blessed your earliest child;

And when to soothe some little wrong
It melts into a mother's song,

The same strange sweetness which in years
Long vanished filled the eyes with tears,

And (even when mirthful) gave always
A pathos to your girlish lays,

Falls, with perchance a deeper thrill,
Upon the breathless listener still.[11]

On April 29 Timrod wrote Sophie a note, enclosing a third and final version of the poem. Two of the new couplets expressed his intensity and intentions.

But I would give my hopes of fame
If I could only light the flame.
. . . .

(Yet if not mine, God grant to me
A grave which you may sometimes see!)[12]

Timrod's campaign would henceforth have to be carried on by correspondence. In May there was a new teaching position to report to, since he had departed Mars Bluff along with the Goodwins. Instead of tutoring, Timrod accepted a job teaching classes in a school at Bluffton, in St. Luke's Parish, Beaufort District. Opened thirty-five years earlier as May River Academy, the school was now under the direction of Scotsman Hugh Train. Most of Train's pupils came from Bluffton and surrounding plantations. A substantial community had grown up where a forty-foot-high bluff overlooked the May River in this southernmost corner of South Carolina. An incorporated town,

Bluffton had many homes and two churches. Traveling from Columbia by rail, Timrod arrived first in Savannah, Georgia. Boarding a steamboat, he made his way downriver, past the imposing brick walls of Fort Pulaski, turning north into Calibogue Sound. The boat entered the May River opposite the inland shore of Hilton Head Island.

Timrod immediately regretted his decision to take the job. "If I could have anticipated the task before me," he complained to Emily, "nothing could have induced me to accept the situation. If I had sought the world over for the place most unsuited to my tastes and habits, I could not have succeeded anywhere so well as I have done in Bluffton." Some of his older students had decided to test their new teacher. "I began school yesterday," he continued, "and the boys set straightway to see of what stuff I was made." Timrod sent one unruly pupil to the headmaster for punishment, and Train—described as "a large and powerful man"—gave the boy a well-deserved whipping. After school Timrod took a walk along the bluff to watch the sunset. Train, anticipating trouble, followed him. Suddenly the delinquent, armed with a stick, confronted Timrod.

"You sir, were the cause of my getting a thrashing this morning, but there's going to be the damnedest thrashing now that ever you saw!"

Before Timrod could react, Train grabbed the bully.

"You are quite right sir," shouted Train, "there is going to be the damnedest thrashing ever heard of, but you are the scoundrel that's going to get it!"

Timrod made no mention to Emily of the thwarted ambush, maintaining that in class he "met every demonstration with a promptness and decision which astonished them very soon into proper behavior. . . . Still all this is disagreeable to me who have always been accustomed to make my pupils my companions. Of course, in a large school like this, it will be improper for me to do anything of the sort . . ." He was glad at least to have one arithmetic class made up of little girls. "I have fixed upon the idlest and most mischievous of them all as my favorite, a Miss Stoney; and next to her stands a good little thing with the interesting name of Carrie Pope."

His mind remained on Sophie. "Give her my love," he told Emily, "yes! say love, if she be not afraid of it burning her . . ." Still, "my dearest hope on earth seems unattainable." Now almost thirty-two, Timrod was in a quandary. "To tell the plain truth," he confessed to his sister, "I was not born to be a teacher; and I expect with my inordinate sensibility to encounter much that will give me acute pain." He wished it were possible to give Train his resignation, but "I am positive that I will not teach after the expiration of this year. If I can't get a Professorship, I must see whether I can't live on a poet's pittance." If he could not have Sophie, "I don't see why I should wish for more." He closed the letter with affection for his family. "Kiss the children for me—bless their dear little hearts! How I miss them!" And he promised to write to Kate Goodwin "as soon as I can muster my spirits."[13]

Over the next few weeks Timrod's tubercular symptoms flared up, but by mid-June he reported "the pain in my chest decreasing daily." He told Emily that "I find everybody here quite kind and attentive." His attitude about Bluffton had improved. As he convalesced, his doctor, neighbors, and the parents of students invited him to dine and provided transportation. "My usual afternoon's exercise however is a walk on the Bluff, or through the wood behind Bluffton."

Most of that letter to his sister was taken up with complaints about Sophie, who had implied that Timrod's health problems were his own fault, "an evidence of weakness," brought on by excessive "passion." "Be a man," she scolded. Timrod was hurt. "I have generally been held to be a man by those who know me," he told Emily. Miss Sosnowski's passions, he concluded, "are no stronger than water or than moonlight." Though affectionate, "I doubt whether that heart of hers will ever throb violently enough to give even the small pain of a headache."

Russell's having ceased publication, Timrod sent his "Two Portraits" manuscript to *Harper's* where it appeared in August before a national audience.[14] Of course only Sophie, the author, and their immediate circle knew for whom it had been written. Timrod continued to be very fond of Sophie and they remained friends. It would be some months before he entirely gave up hope. But she had thwarted a romantic relationship.

꽃 꽃 꽃

Fifteen years earlier the people of Bluffton had welcomed their congressman, Robert Barnwell Rhett, home from Washington with a dinner in his honor. He responded with a speech about the tariff. More than a decade after the Nullification crisis, Federal import duties were again edging upwards. Rhett wanted permanent relief, even if that meant South Carolina's secession from the United States. What became known as the "Bluffton Movement" soon had the state in an uproar, until conservatives gained the upper hand and another compromise tariff reduction emerged. But there were even more threatening storm clouds on the horizon. When the House of Representatives proposed to ban slaves from territories acquired from Mexico, Southerners reacted angrily. Were the territories not the common property of all the states? they asked. Had not Southern blood been shed in the war with Mexico? The Compromise of 1850 proved to be a bitter disappointment. The one concession made by the North—the Fugitive Slave Act—went unenforced. Northern Abolitionists continued to grow in influence, as did the stridency of their demands. New York senator William H. Seward appealed to a "higher law than the Constitution" and spoke of an "irrepressible conflict" with the South. Abraham Lincoln proclaimed that "a house divided" between slaveholding and non-slaveholding states could not stand. It seemed there could be no peace between the sections until the North remade all America in its own image. Such reasoning and rhetoric would have shocked the founding generation.

Then in October 1859 John Brown—who already had a well-earned reputation for terrorism—seized the U. S. Arsenal at Harper's Ferry, Virginia. Secretly financed by prominent Northern Abolitionists, Brown and his band sought to arm blacks and ignite an insurrection. The revolt soon collapsed, but not before innocent blood was shed. Tried in Virginia and hanged for murder, Brown was hailed as a martyr by many in the North. Church bells tolled as Abolitionist clergymen compared him to Jesus, and likened his gallows to the cross of Christ. Conservative Southerners who had heretofore rejected secession now began to question how they could possibly remain yoked with those bent on their destruction.

The Democratic national convention met in Charleston, South Carolina, in April 1860 and quickly broke up over the issue of slavery in the territories. Two separate factions would later nominate candidates for president. The new Constitutional Union party put a contender in the race. Abraham Lincoln, the Republican nominee, faced a splintered opposition. As the presidential campaign progressed, opinion in South Carolina became nearly unanimous. Should Lincoln win—should this sectional party capture the power of the presidency—it would signal the beginning of a revolution and the effective overthrow of the Constitution. In such a circumstance South Carolina would have no choice but to leave a Union dominated by her sworn enemies. As promised, when Lincoln won an electoral college majority (with little more than 39% of the popular vote) South Carolina convened a Convention of the People. That body met in Charleston and on December 20, 1860, voted unanimously for independence. Amid a storm of rejoicing, the state proclaimed itself an independent republic.

Never had South Carolinians been as united. A handful, mostly in the Up-Country, thought the action unwise or premature. But even they rallied to their state once the vote was taken. Nearly the only unionist left in Charleston was lawyer Petigru, a character so liked and respected that all smiled at his eccentricity. "Disabuse your mind of the notion that there is any party, or body of men, in S. C. not willing for secession," Simms wrote to New York editor and friend James Lawson. "There are not a dozen men. The fact is that it is a complete landsturm, a general rising of the people, and the politicians are far behind them." Unionists of an earlier generation, men who like William Henry Timrod battled Calhoun and Nullification, now wore blue secession cockades.[15]

Henry Timrod's first recorded mention of his state's declaration of independence is in a January 1861 letter to his sister. "My dear Emily, give me a good rousing letter when you next write—a little blood and thunder, mixed with original allusions to the Palmetto flag; and then perhaps I may write a song worthy of the occasion and—the people!"[16]

6

"Hath not the morning dawned
with added light?"

As THE PEOPLE REJOICED IN THEIR INDEPENDENCE, TIMROD TRANS-
ferred from the school at Bluffton to a new position in Hardeeville.
Still in Beaufort District, the village was on the line of the Charleston
and Savannah Railroad, just five miles from the state of Georgia. His
new employer was well-to-do physician Joseph Hazel. Dr. Hazel and
wife Mary had two teenaged sons, one preparing for college. There
were probably a few other students also sharing the little schoolhouse, located in pine trees on the outskirts of Hardeeville. "I am
among very good people," Timrod reported, "but far plainer and
less pretending than the Blufftonians. I must say that I should prefer
a little more polish than I have seen yet, but I am ready to overlook
the absence of that in consideration of the really sterling qualities
which supply its place."[1]

At the Hazels' home Timrod read newspaper accounts of rapidly
unfolding events. Each day brought thrilling dispatches. The example of South Carolina was followed during January by Mississippi,
Florida, Alabama, Georgia, Louisiana, and Texas. Delegates from the
seceded states met in the Montgomery, Alabama state capitol beginning February 4. Among South Carolina's eight representatives were
Robert Barnwell Rhett from Colleton District and Orangeburg's
Lawrence Massillon Keitt. All were determined to have a Southern
government in place before Lincoln's inauguration the following
month. They adopted a provisional constitution, chose "Confederate
States of America" as the name of the new nation, and elected Jefferson Davis their president.[2]

Even as he taught, Timrod found time to pen the patriotic poem mentioned to his sister. Mailed to the *Daily Courier* in Charleston, it appeared on February 23 entitled "Ode on Occasion of the Meeting of the Southern Congress." It contained four complex stanzas with irregular length of line and a varying rhyme scheme. Reaction was immediate and electrifying. No Timrod poem had ever received such attention. A broadside was published. Printed and reprinted by other papers across the South, even *The Living Age* of Boston picked it up.[3]

> HATH not the morning dawned with added light?
> And shall not evening call another star
> Out of the infinite regions of the night,
> To mark this day in Heaven? At last, we are
> A nation among nations; and the world
> Shall soon behold in many a distant port
>   Another flag unfurled!
> . . . .
> And what if, mad with wrongs themselves have wrought,
>   In their own treachery caught,
>   By their own fears made bold,
>   And leagued with him of old,
> Who long since in the limits of the North
> Set up his evil throne, and warred with God—
> What if, both mad and blinded in their rage,
> Our foes should fling us down their mortal gage,
> And with a hostile step profane our sod!

Even in that event, the poet is supremely confident of his country's success. The Southern cause is not merely dependent on the courage, resources, and determination of its people. Within the North–South cultural clash is a moral element—a struggle between good and evil—and "To doubt the end were want of trust in God."

> On one side, creeds that dare to teach
> What Christ and Paul refrained to preach;
> Codes built upon a broken pledge,
> And Charity that whets a poniard's edge;
> Fair schemes that leave the neighboring poor

> To starve and shiver at the schemer's door,
> While in the world's most liberal ranks enrolled,
> He turns some vast philanthropy to gold;
> Religion, taking every mortal form
> But that a pure and Christian faith makes warm,
> Where not to vile fanatic passion urged,
> Or not in vague philosophies submerged,
> Repulsive with all Pharisaic leaven,
> And making laws to stay the laws of Heaven!
> And on the other, scorn of sordid gain,
> Unblemished honor, truth without a stain,
> Faith, justice, reverence, charitable wealth,
> And, for the poor and humble, laws which give,
> Not the mean right to buy the right to live,
>   But life, and home, and health!

Timrod shares his vision of a distant future. The Confederate South is destined to become a great nation for the ultimate purpose of blessing the entire world.

> For, to give labor to the poor,
>   The whole sad planet o'er,
> And save from want and crime the humblest door,
> Is one among the many ends for which
>   God makes us great and rich!

Within a year the poem would be published as "Ethnogenesis," the title it would retain. "The dignity and calmness of its tone," said Hayne, "covering unsounded depths of ardor and enthusiasm; its subtle grace of imagination, feeling, and imagery, and the *crisp* purity of the versification are so artistically blended in this ODE, that one cannot criticise, but must simply and honestly admire it."[4]

Hayne wrote Timrod to tell him that his literary friends were unanimous in their praise. Simms sent his own congratulations. Happily too, "I am rejoiced to hear that Miss Sophie is pleased with my ode." The fair sex continued to claim his attention. To sister Emily he mentioned a girl named Lizzie and inquired about Sallie Cannon. "Give my love to her dark eyes," wrote Timrod of Sallie, "and tell her to reserve her sweetest kiss for my lips in April." His young nieces seemed piqued at his words. "There might have been more *warmth* . . . in the [promised] kiss I gave to Sallie than that which I gave to them," but he urged Emily to assure them that "there certainly was less *affection.*"

Within months the hope he once held for winning Sophie was gone. "I love her no longer indeed, but I still feel towards her tenderly enough to wish to save her from the slightest mortification. I shall certainly write to her, and tell her that though she is not the Miss Sophie of my imagination, she is still a very lovable little person, and I shall be glad to have her dearest friendship." Sophie would be courted by Frank Schaller, a young teacher at Hillsborough Military Academy in North Carolina.[5] If Timrod's "Two Portraits" had an influence, it was not precisely that which the poet intended. Sophie soon became Mrs. Frank Schaller.

The North would not let the South depart in peace. On April 13 Confederate artillery forced the surrender of Fort Sumter, where Federals had defied Southern sovereignty by their continued domination of Charleston Harbor. Two days later Lincoln declared war in his call for troops to invade the seceded states. The Upper South responded by joining the Confederacy. Young men of both countries flocked to their colors as battle lines were drawn.

With war on the way, the student Timrod was tutoring postponed plans for college, though the door of the little school probably remained open for a time. "If I could get a situation in some other part of the State," Timrod wrote Emily on June 11, "I should leave Hardeeville at once . . . I am sick of the place and the people—the Hazels, who are very kind and very dull people, being excepted." He fretted for the security of undefended Bluffton, but was relieved to learn that Hilton Head was finally being reinforced. Militia volunteers—men in state, not Confederate service—were rallying for local defense. "A company is forming at Hardeeville and Perrysburg [Purrysburg] which I shall join of course; and even if we are not enough to beat the Yankees off, we shall have at least the satisfaction to die fighting. Still I confess that—if I have to fight, I should rather do it elsewhere, amid the friends of my youth, and among people who know me other than as a poor country schoolmaster, than in this obscure and uncivilized corner."

Coastal South Carolina was as yet untroubled by invading Yankees. But Timrod had fought and lost another kind of battle during visits to Columbia and Charleston the month before. In one letter to a friend he wrote flippantly of being "compelled to drown my sorrow in more than one iced julep." He expressed more contrition in a missive to his sister. "Nothing that you can say, however painful," he told Emily, "can make me regret the past—more deeply than I do already. Let me beseech you, if possible, to put away the memory of the last week I spent with you, and to think of me as I really am." He claimed to have turned over a new leaf. "More solemn thoughts have come to me lately than I have been accustomed to entertain, and in a more serious and resolute mood than I have ever known, I have determined to be pure and temperate." It seems, this time, that he kept his promise.

Another young woman had recently captured his eye. "I received last week a very pleasant letter from Miss Rachel Lyons," he told Emily. Rachel was in her early twenties, intelligent, alluring, fluent in French, and a member of South Carolina's small but distinguished Jewish community. "She is rapidly conquering my old prejudice against the Hebrew," confessed Timrod.

He sent Rachel a copy of his *Poems*, the flyleaf inscribed with twelve lines of "To R. L.," a gallant if conventional dedication. "Put my compliment," he wrote her, "gracefully into your pocket (I *think* ladies have pockets) or rather into your heart (I am *almost sure* they have hearts), and thank me with one of your most deluding smiles!"[6] In the heat of early summer he complained to her of lethargy, but remarked how he delighted to hear the wind in the pines. "There are few sounds which possess a greater charm for me; and I never hear it without being soothed, and, if discontented at the moment, rebuked and softened. What a strange impressiveness (as in whispers about a dead body) it has!" He told Rachel he was searching for the subject of his next poem, so far without success. "There is one theme indeed (An Arctic Voyage) which has haunted me from childhood," he said. On that great work "I wish to stake my hopes of a lasting fame," but only when he felt his abilities had reached full maturity. "Is it not strange that I, born in a semi-tropical country, have been always more attracted by the dark seas and rocky coasts in the vicinity of the Pole, than by the magnificent vegetation and luminous waters of Equatorial regions?"[7]

Timrod described his dreary militia duties. "In my small person, I unite the offices of quartermaster, secretary, treasurer, and Chairman of the 'Committee upon the Constitution and by-laws.'" He regretted that not a man in the company was an "educated gentleman," and again spoke of serving elsewhere. As much as he disliked being a private, "I am so utterly destitute of military knowledge, that I cannot honestly seek a commission." He failed to mention his very real handicaps of ill health and a lack of financial resources. Though the Beaufort coast for now remained quiet, Union and Confederate forces were gathering in Virginia. Timrod noted that his and Rachel's letters thus far contained nothing on the state of the country. "Let us continue to ignore the subject. Each confident of the other's patriotism, we can afford, I think, to dally with pleasanter topics, without incurring mutual suspicions of indifference to the great events going on about us."

Rachel later remembered her friend as being "singularly light-hearted and full of droll mischief. He could gravely argue—in an irresistible flow of words, then suddenly stop laughingly, his lovely gray eyes flashing with fun, and throwing up his hands in mock deprecation (with a gesture entirely his own) would wait to see if you had been deluded by his eloquence into replying derisively."

"You may also look soon for a poem entitled 'The Cotton Boll,'" Timrod told Rachel on August 20, "but where, I cannot tell you— certainly however in the paper which I think will pay me the highest price. Am I not mercenary?"[8] Besides occupying a near-empty schoolhouse and shuffling papers for the Hardeeville militia, Timrod had redeemed his time by writing another memorable poem. In 167 irregular lines and a varied pattern of rhyme, Timrod envisions his country's future. "The Cotton Boll" appeared in the Charleston *Mercury* on September 3.

The poet examines a boll and, unraveling its fibers,

> A veil seems lifted, and for miles and miles
> The landscape broadens on my sight,

Laid out is the beauty of the Southern land, but more, he foresees that the destiny of the Confederacy is to benefit and prosper the world through peaceful trade. "That mighty commerce . . .

> Joins with a delicate web remotest strands;
> And gladdening rich and poor,
> Doth gild Parisian domes,

> Or feed the cottage-smoke of English homes,
> And only bounds its blessings by mankind!

Just a month earlier Confederates had routed Federal invaders at Manassas, Virginia. The South basked in the glory of that first, great triumph. Still, Timrod remembered the cost in lives and feared that even more blood would be spilled before independence was won. He knew "That there is much even Victory must regret."

> Oh, help us, Lord! to roll the crimson flood
> Back on its course, and, while our banners wing
> Northward, strike with us! till the Goth shall cling
> To his own blasted altar-stones, and crave
> Mercy; and we shall grant it, and dictate
> The lenient future of his fate
> There, where some rotting ships and crumbling quays
> Shall one day mark the Port which ruled the Western seas.[9]

Timrod planned other poems that summer in Hardeeville, but told Rachel they would have to await the coming of peace. "The lyre of Tyrtus is the only one to which the Public will listen now," he wrote, alluding to the schoolmaster-poet of ancient Greece who inspired the Spartans to victory. He even tried to write a Southern national anthem, but abandoned the effort. "There seems to be some especial difficulty in writing a song of this nature. There is really not a single good one in the language; for 'Rule Britannica' and 'The Star-Spangled Banner' are both worthless as poetry."[10]

In September Timrod again visited Columbia before traveling to Charleston, his mother's and sister Rebecca's home. "I have but to shut my eyes," he reminisced to Rachel, "to be seated at will either in my sister's parlour with my sister and the children before me, and Kate—at no great distance; or in your home *tête-à-tête* with the . . . 'charmed tongue' of Miss Rachel Lyons!" He had been idle since coming to Charleston. "Except an occasional stroll to the newspaper offices, I have gone *nowhere*." And he remained "unvisited by the Muse"—unable to write any verse.[11] Soon he had a brighter report. "The Goddess knocked at the door of my study last Saturday night [December 21] and handed me a poem entitled 'Katie'! I have sent it to the *Mercury* in the columns of which it will probably appear on Friday."

"Katie" contained 200 lines of iambic tetrameter, without formal grouping in stanzas. It was published in both the *Mercury* and *Daily Courier* on Saturday, December 28.

> It may be through some foreign grace,
> And unfamiliar charm of face;
> It may be that across the foam
> Which bore her from her childhood's home,
> By some strange spell, my Katie brought,
> Along with English creeds and thought—
> Entangled in her golden hair—
> Some English sunshine, warmth, and air!

A glowing tribute and vivid picture of Katie and the land of her birth, the poet went further.

> And soon, despite of storm or calm,
> Beneath my native groves of palm,
> Kind friends shall greet, with joy and pride,
> The Southron and his English bride![12]

Timrod explained himself to Rachel even before the poem was published. "With regard to the *sentiments* which the poem expresses you must give them a very liberal construction. Katie and I are by no means on the lover-like terms implied in my verse. Nor indeed are we likely to become so—the affection between us being much like that which sometimes exists between favourite cousins. If you ask me why then I should address her in so passionate a style, I can only answer that (metrically) I am always in love for the time with the woman who forms the subject of my song. It is a species of temporary hallucination for which I shall not here attempt to account . . ." Katie herself thought that the poem "invested me with attributes I never possessed. Many is the time, that I have urged him to see me as I really was . . ."[13]

His letters to Katie are lost, but a week after the poem appeared Timrod wrote to his sister. "The reports with regard to my engagement with Katie give me little concern," he told Emily, "but I suppose that it will annoy Katie from the fact that it may keep other admirers at a distance. She will scarcely regard, I fear, my poor poem, nor even the affection which it implies, as a complete equivalent for the loss of half a dozen suitors." All South Carolina wanted to know who "Katie" was. "Nobody ever cared to ask me," said the author, "who was the original of 'Two Portraits.'"[14] Rachel told Timrod—after forty days of icy silence—that among her multitude of criticisms she especially did not like the final lines of the poem. "There is no reason why you should hesitate to speak to me with perfect frankness with regard to my productions," he replied. "I can endure any amount of criticism with perfect equanimity." He reiterated that he and Katie were not engaged. "You are grossly mistaken if you think there is any 'unexplored region' in my heart. I know all its roads and byroads better than I know the streets of Charleston. Katie has a pretty little cottage in one of them I acknowledge; but embosomed in the deepest recess of a region known only to myself is a palace which is yet unoccupied. In what enchanted portion of the world slumbers the princess who is to take possession of it, no fortune-teller has ever yet revealed to me."

Timrod had jotted a few lines of verse in the copy of his book given to Rachel ("To R. L."). He had also written a poem on the pages of her diary ("Lines to R. L."). Now, as something of a peace offering, he sent her yet another. Though "perhaps only a *variation* of the same thought" written about Katie, he hoped Rachel would "find it sufficiently distinct from that, to make it worthy of your acceptance."[15] Indeed, she found "La Belle Juive" most acceptable. It first appeared in the *Daily Courier* on January 23, 1862, and was soon published in papers across the South. Its thirteen stanzas were filled with Old Testament allusions.

> The crowd is sauntering at its ease,
> And humming like a hive of bees—
> You take your seat and touch the keys.
>
> I do not hear the giddy throng;
> The sea avenges Israel's wrong,
> And on the wind floats Miriam's song!
> . . . .
> I watch afar the gleaner sweet;
> I wake like Boaz in the wheat,
> And find you lying at my feet!

> My feet! Oh! if the spell that lures
> My heart through all these dreams endures,
> How soon shall I be stretched at yours!

But the search went on for his "princess." In a letter written just after the publication of "La Belle Juive," a most ungallant Timrod told Rachel of "a flirtation which promises quite well." His interest was a comely Charleston girl of eighteen. "Talks well, but sparingly! Listens credulously! Adores Tennyson! And admires me!!"[16]

There were fewer men of military age left on the streets of Charleston for her to admire. Over 27,000 from the state had already gone to war. George Goodwin may have been too unwell to serve, but sister Edith's thirty-six-year-old husband Ainsley H. Cotchett joined the artillery. Timrod was thirty-three in December of 1861. His health, though he was loath to admit it, made him a poor candidate for life in the field. Conscription was on the way, but he could have easily secured a medical exemption. It was obvious that a pen in Timrod's hand was worth far more to the cause than a musket. Still, he felt he should serve in uniform. In mid-December he spoke with "some recruiting friends," and an arrangement was made. He traveled to Orangeburg and on December 21, enlisted in the 20th South Carolina Infantry Regiment. He was sworn in for a twelve-month enlistment by his company commander, Captain Paul A. McMichael. The 20th South Carolina was a new organization and the recruits of McMichael's Company B were training at Camp Hampton near Columbia. The commanding officer of the regiment—Colonel Lawrence Massillon Keitt—wanted Timrod as his secretary and had even offered him the use of a horse. Since Keitt's command was still mobilizing, Timrod's clerical duties were not yet needed and he was allowed to return home.[17] He had expressed the hope that he might qualify for an officer's commission. "I am afraid that after all I must go to the wars as a private," he told Rachel. "My utter want of military knowledge prevents me asking a position with the impudence necessary to obtain one." There were all too many officers, on both sides, with impudence and few skills. More cogent considerations were the state of Timrod's health and his inability to afford an officer's uniform, arms, and equipage.

During February Colonel Keitt was on James Island, south of Charleston, preparing for the deployment of his regiment. Timrod expected to join him, he told Rachel on February 4, "as soon as I am perfectly well." Apparently tuberculosis was hampering him again. He hoped to "pay a brief visit to Columbia before going permanently into camp. I don't like the idea of subjecting myself to the risks of a campaign without one more pressure of Katie's hand, and one more glance into Miss Rachel's eyes." He would not admit it to "la belle juive," but he could not now afford even the expense of this short trip. To make matters worse, in mid-February he was thrown from a buggy as he rode to the Charleston Race Course where the regiment then camped. His back and side were severely bruised, bed rest again delaying active duty. On March 1 Timrod reported to Captain McMichael at the Race Course and—in compliance with new Confederate legislation—reenlisted to serve for the duration of the war. Again he was excused from duty, listed as being "on detached service."[18]

Private Timrod would strike more blows for his country as a civilian. The Southern cause had met with a series of setbacks after the initial triumphs of the previous summer. There were defeats in the West. Britain and France withheld recognition. "We have over bid the power of King Cotton," admitted the author of "The Cotton Boll." "When King Wheat gets upon his throne, he is just as strong." In November a Union invasion force captured Port Royal and Hilton Head Island, South Carolina. "I am afraid that most of us are too easily prone to be discouraged," Timrod told his sister in February. "What looks darkest in our course at present is the ease with which the people seem to be depressed by reverses. In this respect we may learn a lesson even from the Yankees. All their defeats of last year have only nerved them to their stupendous efforts in this."[19]

Near the first of February he wrote "A Cry to Arms." It was a patriotic if commonplace appeal, aimed at those who had found reasons to delay going into the service of their country. He sent a copy to Rachel on February 6, mentioning that he was holding on to "another and far better poem." Though he regretted the necessity of doing so, he sought again to strike the best possible bargain with a newspaper. He was strapped for cash.

The *Daily Courier* must have won the bidding, for his "far better poem" found a place in its columns on March 8, 1862. The title was "Carolina." Directed at the people of his own state, its twenty-one stanzas expressed with galvanizing intensity a resolve to conquer or die.

THE despot treads thy sacred sands,
Thy pines give shelter to his bands,
Thy sons stand by with idle hands,
           Carolina!

He breathes at ease thy airs of balm,
He scorns the lances of thy palm;
Oh! who shall break thy craven calm,
           Carolina!

. . . .

I hear a murmur as of waves
That grope their way through sunless caves,
Like bodies struggling in their graves,
           Carolina!

And now it deepens; slow and grand
It swells, as, rolling to the land,
An ocean broke upon the strand,
           Carolina!

Shout! let it reach the startled Huns!
And roar with all thy festal guns!
It is the answer of thy sons,
           Carolina!

. . . .

Ere thou shalt own the tyrant's thrall
Ten times ten thousand men must fall;
Thy corpse may hearken to his call,
           Carolina!

When by thy bier in mournful throngs
The women chant thy mortal wrongs,
'T will be their own funereal songs,
           Carolina!

From thy dead breast by ruffians trod
No helpless child shall look to God;
All shall be safe beneath thy sod,
           Carolina![20]

Paul Hayne was then stationed as an artillery officer at Fort Sumter. There, on a stormy March evening, he first read Timrod's ex-

traordinary new poem. The impression it had on him was unforget-
table. "Walking along the battlements, under the red light of a tem-
pestuous sunset, the wind steadily and loudly blowing from off the
bar across the tossing and moaning waste of waters, driven inland;
with scores of gulls and white sea-birds flying and shrieking round
me,—those wild voices of Nature mingled strangely with the rhyth-
mic roll and beat of the poet's impassioned music."[21]

7

"On detached service"

LINCOLN DECLARED A BLOCKADE OF THE SOUTHERN COAST EARLY IN
the war, though months would pass before it became effective. By the
spring of 1862 Charleston was under threat from enemy forces based
at Port Royal. Major General John C. Pemberton assumed command
of regional Confederate defenses on March 14 and immediately created an outcry by ordering a series of retreats all along the South Carolina coast. Consolidating the lines was his objective. Brigadier General Roswell S. Ripley protested in vain as artillery was removed from
forward positions on Coles Island. As Ripley predicted, Union gun-
boats began steaming unmolested up the Stono River and soon Folly
Island and Johns Island were overrun by Federals. James Island, adja-
cent to Charleston, was in danger. The men of the 20th South Carolina Infantry Regiment were now more needed than ever.

There would be a strengthening of Charleston's naval defenses as
well. Early that year the state appropriated $300,000 for the con-
struction of an ironclad warship, but the Confederate government
stepped in and assumed the expense. The vessel would be chris-
tened the *Chicora*. A female letter-writer to the Charleston *Daily
Courier* then challenged the women of South Carolina to pay for the
construction of an additional armored ship. The response was enthusiastic. Women and children, rich and poor—even blacks—raised
funds to build the *Palmetto State*. "We are only children," read a letter
published in April, "but anxious to contribute our mite towards the
Palmetto gunboat fund. We enclose $16, the proceeds of the raffle of
two articles of jewelry, precious to us as the gifts of valued friends,
but cheerfully given to the holy cause of Southern liberty." The letter
was signed by Edith and Anna Goodwin.[1]

"I still stand hesitating upon the brink before plunging into camp life," Timrod wrote to Rachel Lyons on Tuesday, April 8. In but two days he planned to board a boat at the Charleston battery that would take him to regimental headquarters on James Island. He was encouraged by reported strengthening of local defenses and heartened by the "glorious news from the West." Initial dispatches told of victory at Pittsburg Landing, Tennessee, near a little house of worship called Shiloh Church. As he wrote to Rachel a warm breeze blew in his open window, "sporting with my papers, and playing through my hair like a caressing hand!" This day his mood matched the spring sunshine. "Owing to a naturally melancholy disposition, and my own follies, I have been for the most part of my life a rather miserable dog. But better times, and a better spirit are coming . . ."

What he was unwilling to tell Rachel was that he and Katie—probably during a brief visit to Columbia on April first—had come to an understanding. There was no formal announcement of an engagement nor was a date set. But, all of Timrod's protestations to the contrary, Katie Goodwin was the one he had asked to marry him. And she had at least tentatively accepted.[2] Perhaps "Katie" had been his way of proposing. Without their correspondence we can only speculate. Timrod did not want to lose Rachel's friendship, but he must have gradually come to understand that he had even less chance of winning her than Sophie. Women certainly found Timrod's wit and attentiveness appealing. All admired his extraordinary gifts as a writer. But Rachel, like Sophie, came from a solid middle-class family while Timrod struggled daily with literal poverty. Winning the hand of Katie Goodwin, orphan in an adopted country, may have seemed a more attainable goal.

Just as Timrod was about to report to Colonel Keitt he received an offer of civilian employment. Months earlier he had mentioned the possibility of "being appointed on the editorial staff of a certain important paper as soon as my [military] campaign is over." Now the *Mercury*, edited by Robert Barnwell Rhett, Jr., asked him to become a war correspondent with the army in the West. Timrod was offered a generous $6 per day (nearly half the *monthly* pay for an army private) plus traveling expenses. His regimental commander was most willing for Timrod to accept, still officially listing the private as "on detached service."[3]

Colonel Keitt, General Ripley, and editor Rhett all penned letters of introduction for Timrod to take to General P. G. T. Beauregard. Keitt addressed another letter to his friend Major General George B. Crittenden. Timrod would depart Charleston by rail on the afternoon of April 15. His destination was Corinth, Mississippi, where Beauregard had retreated with his army. Success on the first day of battle at Shiloh ended in defeat on the next, after Albert Sidney Johnston, the Confederate commander, was killed. The North lost 13,047 men in the two-day struggle; Southern casualties totaled 10,694. It was the deadliest battle yet fought in America.

Timrod was apprehensive. "I accept this mission with fear and trembling," he told Emily, despite Rhett's assurance "that all doors will fly open before my reputation." Brother-in-law George Goodwin gently intimated to Timrod that he lacked "shrewdness." Timrod thought he needed not shrewdness but "the 'brass' to make use of it." He confessed to Rachel that a "want of *savoir-faire*, and my comparative inability to make my way among strangers will put many difficulties in my way." He expected to experience "great hardships" and see "shocking sights" at the battlefront. Surely he was mindful too of the fact that as a soldier in civilian dress he was subject to execution if he fell into enemy hands and his status was discovered. "Beauregard's position is a difficult one," he wrote his sister on the day of his departure. Were Confederates again defeated, "I can look forward to nothing but death or capture." He had a powerful new motivation. "But for my engagement with Katie I would have preferred to remain idle in Keitt's camp. But I owe it to the dear girl to show that I have energy and a capacity. . . . Katie is my inspiration and my strength—(please let her see this letter—I believe I omitted to tell her this in my epistle to her)—and with the hope of marrying her, I feel that there are no obstacles which I am not ready to encounter."

With tears in his eyes he expressed to Emily a brother's love. "Kiss the dear children for me—let me name them all—Kate, Edith, bright little Anna and Harry—all of them as precious to me as if they were my own." He departed, relying "on your prayers and Katie's, Ma's and Rebecca's to protect me."[4]

The first leg of Timrod's journey ended in Atlanta. The most direct route to Corinth would have been to transfer to the Charleston and Memphis Railroad in Chattanooga, Tennessee, but the Yankees had cut that line.[5] A circuitous route would be required, south and then west to Montgomery, Alabama. There would be travel by road and water before boarding a train of the Mobile and Ohio Railroad for the trip north through the Magnolia State. Corinth, in the northeastern corner of Mississippi, was strategically located at the junction of two railroad lines. Certainly the farthest Timrod had ever been away from home, the town was about seventeen miles southwest of the Shiloh battlefield.

Corinth was in chaos. Thousands of wounded soldiers crowded the town. Contaminated water led to an outbreak of typhoid. Soon Beauregard would report that 18,000 of his troops were absent, sick. "I am still unable to predict the precise hour when the struggle is to begin," wrote Timrod in his first dispatch to the *Mercury* on May 1. "I hear nothing on the part of the soldiers but confidence in their power to drive the invaders back." He had arrived in Corinth accompanied by men of the 10th South Carolina Infantry Regiment. These troops had guarded Georgetown in their home state until transferred to the Army of Mississippi. He complimented them on their military bearing and excellent behavior. "Here, in the woods of the Mississippi, the bayonets of the palm will be found no less sharp than where they fight the winds or defy the tyrant upon the Atlantic coast."

War correspondent Timrod filed his reports under the *nom de plume* "Kappa." His choice of the tenth letter of the Greek alphabet may have been a salute to his traveling companions. Though able to gather little hard news, his pen was extraordinarily descriptive. "I have seldom seen a more beautiful sky than that under which Corinth reposed last night," he wrote on Tuesday, May 6.

> The moon is still young, yet the heavens were bathed with a tender light, in which there was that barely perceptible flush which is only to be observed in a southern clime. The night, too, was unusually quiet; not a sound was to be heard, except the occasional fall of a voice from a watchfire hard by, or now and then the pastoral tinkle of a cow-bell from a neighboring green. I was at my window enjoying the tranquil time, and musing, of course dreaming of home, when, after a brief while, the strains of a band of music broke upon the silence. They came from a party serenading Beauregard.

It was Beauregard's intention to keep the enemy confused. Timrod and other reporters may have been in close proximity to the army commander, but Beauregard would not share his plans with the press. "Morning after morning, and night after night, one hears the same conflicting rumors, hopes, fears, doubts, arguments and speculations," wrote "Kappa." One story Beauregard did hope would reach Union general Henry Halleck was that Confederates were about to go on the offensive. Though outnumbered two to one, Southern troops were ordered to prepare for just such an action. At the last minute—with the enemy more cautious than ever—Beauregard's army fell back fifty miles to the safety of Tupelo, Mississippi.[6]

Timrod fell back too, riding the train south all the way to Mobile, Alabama. By now he was suffering again from tubercular symptoms and questioning his ability to continue as a correspondent. At the home of author and prominent Mobile resident Octavia Le Vert, one observed that "on rare occasions the pale, worn face of Henry Timrod was seen in their quieter corners." At Le Vert's Timrod met James Ryder Randall, author of "My Maryland"—one of the South's most stirring war lyrics. "He was essaying the difficult role of war correspondent," remembered Randall, "but his mind was unfitted for such rude employment and 'dwelt among the stars.' He could hardly travel any distance without losing his valise; and he had that singular disease which makes one blind or nearly so at night. I had to carry him around, at dusk, as if he were sightless. Even in those days he was not robustly fitted . . ." Timrod made his way to Columbia in June. "Out of the refluent tides of blood, from under the smoke of conflict, and the sickening fumes of slaughter," wrote Hayne, "he staggered homeward, half blinded, bewildered, with a dull red mist before his eyes, and a shuddering horror at heart."[7]

It may have been about this time that Timrod received the sobriquet "Poet Laureate of the Confederate South." A newspaper reported the laureate "now prostrate on a bed of sickness. Severe hemorrhages of a dangerous character have laid him down, but we hope ere long that gentle nursing will restore him once more to his accustomed health and haunts." He retreated to the Columbia home of sister Emily to be healed of what one called his "shattered nerves and wrecked constitution."[8]

By the middle of the month Timrod had recovered sufficiently to visit Mary Chesnut's Columbia cottage. On this evening Paul Hayne was there, along with Louisa Bartow, widow of Colonel Francis S. Bartow. Telegraphic reports had been received that day of a desperate battle on James Island near a settlement called Secessionville.

Outnumbered and surprised by an early morning attack, Confederates had beaten off the Union assault. "Timrod and Paul Hayne were
discussing this battle tonight with eager excitement," Chesnut recorded in her journal. Timrod's regiment was now stationed on Sul-
livan's Island and not involved in the Secessionville fight. But he and
Hayne both knew that the heroic troops on James Island had saved
Charleston. "Oh," said Mrs. Bartow, "I hope each of them will give us
a poem on it."[9]

Mrs. Chesnut had other guests in July, after Timrod left town for
Charleston. "The beautiful Jewess Rachel Lyons was here today," recounted the diarist. "She flattered Paul Hayne so audaciously. And
he threw back the ball." Mary suspected that Rachel had even set a
coquette's eyes on her own middle-aged husband. "She gave Paul
Hayne the benefit of her philosophy," continued Mary. "Married or
single, all men were alike to her." Rachel went on to disclose her
strategies for flirtation, much to the embarrassment of her friend
Miriam Cohen. Rachel complained, wrote Mary Chesnut, that "Timrod would not introduce her to Paul Hayne; he dreaded her liking
Paul best. And that thought was more than he could bear."[10]

Timrod saw Rachel but briefly in Columbia during June before
she left to visit Richmond and he returned to Charleston. He regretted that they had never been able to meet alone as "I had so much to
say to you which I do not care to put upon paper." No doubt his relationship with Katie needed explaining. "I am advised by my physician not to return to camp," he continued, "but in the absence of all
employment, what else can I do?" The July weather in Charleston
was so oppressive that even the slightest breeze "seems as if it had tra-
versed sands that would burn the feet of the devil himself." Though
he felt unable to write poetry, "I cannot consent, while so many better men than myself are enduring the hardships of a campaign, to
'lay on the roses, and feed on the lilies of life.'" He claimed to have
no immediate plans to visit Columbia. Enclosed in the letter to
Rachel were copies of two poems—"An Exotic" and "Field Flowers"—published by the *Mercury* in July. Both were inspired by Katie.
Once again he cautioned Rachel to keep in mind "that a poet has a
right to idealize, and a lover to be hyperbolical."[11]

Sometime that summer Timrod terminated employment with the
Mercury even as his health forced him to finally abandon any further
thought of army service. Admirers encouraged him to write. John R.

Thompson, formerly editor of the *Southern Literary Messenger*, kept in touch. Thompson had connections with literary men in Great Britain. Friends of Timrod in Charleston, probably with the help of Thompson and others, began to outline plans for the publication of a new edition of Timrod's poetry. Their intention, said Hayne, was to present Timrod "in the highest style, before the world, and at the same time to secure to him a modest competence." They envisioned a handsomely-illustrated volume. Published in London, such a work might also be expected to influence opinion overseas in favor of the Confederate cause. Timrod, at this point, mustered little optimism. "I have a few strong and influential friends who will probably make some exertions in my behalf," he wrote Rachel, "but such has been the ill luck that has pursued me through life, that I do not expect anything but disappointment."[12]

On December 3, 1862, army physician Wilfred DuPont certified that Private Henry Timrod had appeared before the Medical Examining Board and was found to be "incapable of performing the duties of a soldier" due to "Tubercular Phthisis." Their recommended discharge was signed by Captain McMichael on December 8, Timrod's thirty-fourth birthday. His entire year on the roll of Company B of the 20th South Carolina Volunteer Infantry Regiment had been spent "on detached service." During those twelve months he received no army pay.[13]

In December the *Mercury* published Timrod's "Ripley," a poem written to honor the commanding general of Charleston's First Military District. An Ohioan, Ripley was a West Point graduate, Mexican War veteran, and career soldier who had married a Charleston girl. When war came he soon rose to the rank of brigadier general in the Southern army.[14]

"Charleston" appeared in the columns of the *Mercury* on December 3. In Timrod's tribute to a city and a people under siege, his words evoke vivid images.

> No Calpe frowns from lofty cliff or scar
>   To guard the holy strand;
> But Moultrie holds in leash her dogs of war
>   Above the level sand.
>
> And down the dunes a thousand guns lie couched,
>   Unseen, beside the flood—

Like tigers in some Orient jungle crouched
    That wait and watch for blood.
. . . .

Shall the spring dawn, and she still clad in smiles,
    And with an unscathed brow,
Rest in the strong arms of her palm-crowned isles,
    As fair and free as now?

We know not; in the temple of the Fates
    God has inscribed her doom;
And, all untroubled in her faith, she waits
    The triumph or the tomb.[15]

By Christmas of 1862 the bells had been removed from the steeple
of St. Michael's Church and packed off to Columbia for safekeeping.
Thousands of young men were now dead, many in unmarked graves
far from home. Timrod wondered how the city he had known all his
life—indeed, how the whole of the embattled South—should cele-
brate a wartime Yule. His poem "Christmas" came out in the *Mercury*
that day.

How grace this hallowed day?
Shall happy bells, from yonder ancient spire,
Send their glad tidings to each Christmas fire
    Round which the children play?

Alas! for many a moon,
That tongueless tower hath cleaved the Sabbath air,
Mute as an obelisk of ice aglare
    Beneath an Arctic noon.

Shame to the foes that drown
Our psalms of worship with their impious drum,
The sweetest chimes in all the land lie dumb
    In some far rustic town.
. . . .

How could we bear the mirth,
While some loved reveler of a year ago
Keeps his mute Christmas now beneath the snow,
    In cold Virginian earth?

How shall we grace the day?
Ah! let the thought that on this holy morn
The Prince of Peace—the Prince of Peace was born,
    Employ us, while we pray!

Timrod dreams of peace, yearns for peace, cries out for peace. His prayer is not merely for deliverance from the war, but for hearts "all untroubled" by even internal conflict. Yet the poet is no pacifist. The peace he craves—the "Peace wheresoe'er our starry garland gleams" —will only come with the winning of his country's independence.

    Oh ponder what it means!
Oh turn the rapturous thought in every way!
Oh give the vision and the fancy play,
    And shape the coming scenes!

    Peace in the quiet dales,
Made rankly fertile by the blood of men;
Peace in the woodland, and the lonely glen,
    Peace in the peopled vales!

    Peace in the crowded town,
Peace in a thousand fields of waving grain,
Peace in the highway and the flowery lane,
    Peace on the wind-swept down!

    Peace on the farthest seas,
Peace in our sheltered bays and ample streams,
Peace wheresoe'er our starry garland gleams,
    And peace in every breeze![16]

8

"Chance for a while shall seem to reign"

As the proposed British edition of Timrod's poems began to appear practicable, the poet himself became enthusiastic. George A. Trenholm, a wealthy Charleston banker and adviser to the Confederate government, backed the project. City businessman Theodore D. Wagner, known as a patron of literature, stood ready to help. Timrod selected what he considered his best work. Rather than submit a handwritten manuscript to a London publisher, he had a Charleston firm produce typeset proof sheets. When the time came, they would run it through the blockade. "I suppose you have heard that my friends are going to bring out in London a magnificently illustrated edition of my poems," he wrote to niece Edith with justifiable pride. "I am engaged today, and will be engaged for a week in reading the proofs of the copies which are to be sent to England."[1]

Chosen to illustrate the book was Frank Vizetelly, sketch artist for the *Illustrated London News*. Vizetelly came from a family of journalists and had depicted battles in Sardinia and Sicily during the campaigns of Giuseppe Garibaldi. Sent to cover the war in America, Vizetelly followed the U. S. Army in Virginia, North Carolina, Tennessee, and Missouri. In February of 1863 he registered at the Charleston Hotel on Meeting Street, presented his credentials to Generals Ripley and Beauregard (the new commander at Charleston), and quickly went to work drawing local scenes. Since the outbreak of hostilities the artist had made several trips back and forth to England. His sketches were not always so fortunate, some showing up in *Harper's Weekly* after confiscation by Federal blockaders. About the same age as Timrod, Vizetelly was animated and amiable. He loved to tell stories while mimicking the voices of his characters.[2]

One of the new poems to be included in the British edition was written for the opening of a theater in Richmond. Poets were invited to submit dedicatory works to be read on the occasion and the best would receive a $100 prize. John R. Thompson was connected with the competition and in one letter left Timrod with the impression that he had won. Timrod's 126-line poem was well received when read there by an actor, but Paul Hayne's emerged the winner. Despite the difficulty of writing verse "rather rhetorical than poetical," Timrod attempted to encourage a people preoccupied with war. The title was, "Address Delivered at the Opening of the New Theatre at Richmond: A Prize Poem." The stage might, in Timrod's view, provide both a retreat from the struggle and a place where art touches life.

> Love, hate, grief, joy, gain, glory, shame, shall meet,
> As in the round wherein our lives are pent;
>   Chance for a while shall seem to reign,
> While Goodness roves like Guilt about the street
>   And Guilt looks innocent.
> But all at last shall vindicate the right,
> Crime shall be meted with its proper pain,
> Motes shall be taken from the doubter's sight,
> And Fortune's general justice rendered plain.
> . . . .
> Meanwhile, with that calm courage which can smile
> Amid the terrors of the wildest fray,
> Let us among the charms of Art awhile
>   Fleet the deep gloom away;
> Nor yet forget that on each hand and head
> Rest the dear rights for which we fight and pray.[3]

In April Timrod published "Spring" in the *Southern Illustrated News*.

> SPRING, with that nameless pathos in the air
> Which dwells with all things fair,
> Spring, with her golden suns and silver rain,
> Is with us once again.
>
> Out in the lonely woods the jasmine burns
> Its fragrant lamps, and turns

Into a royal court with green festoons
The banks of dark lagoons.

In the deep heart of every forest tree
The blood is all aglee,
And there's a look about the leafless bowers
As if they dreamed of flowers.

Spring was the time when armies must again go on the offensive, and Timrod recoils at coupling "thoughts of war and crime/With such a blessed time!"

Oh! standing on this desecrated mould,
Methinks that I behold,
Lifting her bloody daisies up to God,
Spring kneeling on the sod,

And calling with the voice of all her rills
Upon the ancient hills,
To fall and crush the tyrants and the slaves
Who turn her meads to graves.[4]

Having spent the war primarily on the home front, Timrod understood that

TWO armies stand enrolled beneath
The banner with the starry wreath;

His "The Two Armies" was published in the *Daily South Carolinian* of Columbia in May, and quickly copied by other papers. The poet salutes the Southern woman as she nurses the wounded, encourages the troops,

And, by a thousand peaceful deeds,
Supplies a struggling nation's needs.

Timrod looks forward to the day when "triumph grasped, and freedom won,"

Both armies, from their toils at rest,
Alike may claim the victor's crest.

> But each shall see its dearest prize
> Gleam softly from the other's eyes.[5]

In the spring of 1863 the dream of Southern independence seemed nearer than ever to realization. On April 7 a mighty fleet of U. S. Navy warships, clad with iron and brandishing some of the largest guns ever made, steamed into Charleston Harbor. Navy brass were intent on succeeding where the Union army had failed: by smashing Confederate defenses and taking the city. In hours it was over. Southern gunners drove them off, inflicting unprecedented damage to the armored vessels. After the battle the turret of one Yankee ironclad was said to resemble "an upside-down colander." In Virginia Robert E. Lee's army—though outnumbered more than two to one—surprised and rolled up the enemy flank in a daring attack on the second of May. Chancellorsville, one of the most brilliant victories in military history, prepared the way for Lee's summer invasion of the United States. Two weeks later in Mississippi Union commander Ulysses S. Grant ordered his troops to make a frontal assault on Confederates defending Vicksburg. The bluecoats were bloodily repulsed.

Timrod celebrated his nation's victories in "Carmen Triumphale." Thankful, he was yet mindful of the cost.

> And him, whose heart still weak from fear
>   Beats all too gayly for the time,
>   Know that intemperate glee is crime
> While one dead hero claims a tear.
>
> Yet go thou forth, my song! and thrill,
>   With sober joy, the troubled days;
>   A nation's hymn of grateful praise
> May not be hushed for private ill.
>
> Our foes are fallen! Flash, ye wires!
>   The mighty tidings far and nigh!
>   Ye cities! write them on the sky
> In purple and in emerald fires![6]

Southern faith was again sorely tried when spring's military successes were followed by disheartening reverses. Lee's Army of North-

ern Virginia was defeated at Gettysburg, Pennsylvania, though able
to escape to fight again. The besieged and starving defenders of
Vicksburg were forced to surrender on July 4. And after weeks of
hellish fighting Confederates evacuated the sands of Morris Island at
the mouth of Charleston Harbor.

Timrod's mother and sister Rebecca fled to Columbia. At the
height of the excitement over the struggle for Morris Island, volunteer units of old men and boys mustered in the city. Should the
enemy break through, Charlestonians were determined to fight for
their city street by street. Timrod, for the third time during the war,
stepped forward. "Alas!" he wrote Rachel Lyons, "I soon found my
abilities unequal to my will; a day's service sufficed to convince me
that I was unable to discharge the duties I had undertaken. With a
hemorrhage hardly staunched, I stated my case to my Captain who at
once counseled me to withdraw from the company. I did so, and am
now once more a useless citizen. How very little the country will have
owed me at the conclusion of this war!"[7]

Fitzgerald Ross, English observer of the conflict, arrived in Charleston by rail late on the evening of August 6, as the fighting still
raged on Morris Island. He checked into the Mills House Hotel and
there met artist Vizetelly. After dinner they made their way to the
battery to watch shells "blazing through the air like meteors" around
Fort Sumter. Charleston held. But with the capture of Morris Island,
enemy cannon for the first time were brought within range of the
city. Just after midnight on Saturday, August 22, a Yankee gun,
dubbed the "Swamp Angel," began lobbing explosives into down-
town. Ross was awakened by a "whizzing sound" as the first missile
arced earthward. Vizetelly ran the few blocks from his room at the
Charleston Hotel. The eight-inch-diameter shell had slammed into a
nearby house. Again the pair found their way to the battery "where a
multitude had assembled. We could hear the whiz of the shells long
before they passed over our heads." The bombing went on night and
day. Just a few steps from St. Michael's Church, Ross thought his own
hotel the safest in town. After all, since enemy gunners were aiming
at the steeple, the Englishmen thought it most unlikely they could
score a "bull's-eye shot at 9,000 yards."[8]

Timrod again met with the man who was to illustrate his volume
of verse, though no record remains of what he and Vizetelly said.
About the same time a Confederate artillery officer and *littérateur,*

William Gordon McCabe, became acquainted with Timrod. "Very pleasant he is in conversation," recorded the lieutenant in his journal. "He is a small, melancholy-looking man, black moustache, grey eyes and sallow complexion." Timrod told McCabe that he worked as an editor with the *Mercury,* a job he had accepted just weeks before.[9]

Vizetelly and Ross were again in Charleston in early November, this time on their way to Richmond. They met and socialized with friends they had made in the city, including Timrod. Ross described Timrod, for publication, as "a gentleman whose name has not yet spread as widely as it undoubtedly will do; but he writes beautiful poetry, which no one who has read it can fail to admire."[10] But for whatever reason, the publishing venture languished. Timrod did not understand why. No reason was given. "The great plan," he wrote to Hayne, "for publishing an illustrated edition of my poems has (*I believe*) evaporated in smoke!" No one person seemed to be in charge. The blockade had become very tight. Money was solicited, but Timrod's major backers may simply have had more pressing matters to attend to as the Confederacy's situation became increasingly critical. Hayne remembered how "his once bright anticipations grew duller, until ultimately they smouldered out, one by one, in the anguish, solitude, and bitterness of his soul." Especially disappointed, said Hayne, was the poet's mother. In late 1863 a frustrated Timrod, in a mood of "disgust and despair," handed William McCabe the proof sheets he had prepared, telling the lieutenant that it was "the only copy in the world." The fact that Timrod retained one other set may indicate that his hopes were not yet entirely extinguished.[11]

In July he told Rachel of having "knocked at every door for work in vain." The next month, after a short trip to Columbia, he reported to her his new editorial job with the Charleston *Mercury.* He claimed to be doing the work required of two men at the *Courier,* "to collect facts and to reduce them into form and proportions." It was not a position "best suited to my taste and habits; but I am perfectly willing to do anything which will help to make me independent." Sultry weather and the pressure of newspaper deadlines left him with neither the time nor inclination to write poetry. "The muse does not fly [in] this hot weather. July, August and September are left out of my poetical year." He asked for her encouragement, as "my spirit has become a Dead Sea into which no Jordan flows."

He confided now in Rachel as a friend. There were no more se-
crets to be kept from her about his relationship with Kate Goodwin.
Katie had seen Rachel at a Columbia social gathering and written
Timrod that she was "by far the most beautiful woman in the room."
Timrod repeated the compliment to Rachel. "I can easily believe
Katie's statement; she knows though *you* don't, how lovely I think
you are." He now felt free to share with Rachel his dreams and
hopes—and frustrations—about marriage. "I don't know how you
would regard it; but to me the situation which I am now placed in—
betrothed to a charming girl whom I love with all my heart, and
whom notwithstanding, from the poverty of my circumstances, impossible for me to marry—is a profound grief. Destroy this acknowl-
edgement as soon as you have read it," he said in closing, "for
though I trust you will understand and sympathize with the confes-
sion, others perhaps would only smile at it."[12]

Fortune, in the person of Theodore D. Wagner, was about to
smile once more on Timrod. The *Daily South Carolinian* of Columbia, owned by Dr. Robert W. Gibbes, was being sold to Felix Gregory
De Fontaine and Company. Wagner—an early backer of the London edition project—now arranged for Timrod to join the staff of
the newspaper as associate editor. In addition, the Charleston businessman secured for Timrod a part-ownership. As if that were not
enough, Wagner also handed him several thousand dollars! Though
the purchasing power of Confederate currency had declined, it was
money Timrod could live on and he promptly put it in the bank.[13]

Timrod was to assume his new duties on January 12, 1864. In the
meantime he traveled to Columbia to deliver a lecture. Entitled "A
Theory of Poetry," his presentation was given at a public hall as part
of a benefit for soldiers. Of course Katie was in the audience.

Far longer than his published essays, Timrod's lecture further ex-
pounded and broadened his romantic views of the nature of poetry.
He began by disagreeing with Poe's dictum that true poetry must be
brief enough to read at one sitting. Timrod pointed out that, for example, what little there was in *Paradise Lost* that was *not* true poetry
was still "so raised above the ordinary level of prose" as to harmonize
and not harm the work's unity. Even as a poem could qualify as a
work of art without being entirely poetical, so might poetry itself be
found outside the written word. It was when standing "in the presence of Truth, Power, and Beauty, that I recognize what we all agree
to call Poetry." Timrod held too

that Poetry may develop itself in various modes—in Painting, Sculpture, Architecture, Music, as well as in words. Indeed there is no divining in what quarter this subtle and ethereal spirit may *not* make its appearance. . . . We are talking with a lovely, intelligent woman who assures us that she has no expression for the Poetry that is in her, and afterwards proceeds to recount [the] story of some noble martyrdom, when behold! in the proud flush that mantles her forehead, and the smile that comes up from the depth of her beautiful eyes, the visible presence of Poetry itself.

Filled with pride and confidence, as Timrod left the podium he handed the pages of his lecture to Katie.[14] He had a new job, a part interest in the business, and money in the bank. It was time that he and Katie got married. As if to crown the month, Paul Hayne's poetic tribute, "Sonnet—Addressed to Henry Timrod, Esq.," appeared in the *Daily Courier.*

> Bold Minstrel! earnest patriot! who shall say,
> Albeit thine arm against our general foe,
> In open strife, hath dealt no mortal blow,
> Thou hast not borne thee nobly in the fray,
> Thy mind's impetuous cohorts, thine array,
> Of passionate fancies, feelings grand and high
> Have striven where thoughts ethereal fly,
> On many a well fought field and glorious day!
> The kindling muse hath pealed her clarion song
> O'er land and ocean! souls of faltering will
> Leap to the stormy music, and are strong—
> While the roused pulses of the popular heart
> Swayed by the magic of thy conquering skill,
> Attest the electric energy of Art! [15]

9

"We May Not Falter"

Kate Goodwin and Henry Timrod planned their wedding as he hurried to his desk in the office of the *Daily South Carolinian*. The paper published a tri-weekly edition for rural readers and a weekly digest called the *Portfolio*. There was no Monday edition of the *Carolinian*, allowing the staff a day of rest on the Sabbath. Their building stood on the south side of Washington Street, near Richardson (now Main). Felix G. De Fontaine, pen name "Personne," was editor. The independent-minded Julian A. Selby ran the press and made not a few editorial decisions himself. Selby had been with the paper for two decades. Each owned a greater share in the company than did Timrod, though he soon found himself responsible for nearly every editorial, review, and item of local news. He reprinted much poetry. Timrod's duties would permit almost no time for composing his own verse, but he launched his editorial tenure with the publication of "We May Not Falter," a sonnet encouraging his countrymen in their struggle.[1]

Not every column was occupied with the war. On Saturday morning, January 16, 1864, Timrod shared his down-to-earth insight in "Tact and Talent Compared." He would have his readers understand that tact—self-possessed assurance—"is not a seventh sense, but is the life of all the five . . . Talent is power—tact is skill; talent is weight —tact is momentum; talent knows what to do—tact knows how to do it . . . For all the practical purposes of life, tact carries it against talent—ten to one." In another column he tried to avoid giving offense in cautioning those who might submit original poetry for publication. Even the writer of bad verse, if led by genuinely felt emotion, "ought to be treated with great gentleness. Yet, at the same time, we would advise all in whom the *aura divina* is wanting, to suppress their productions . . . There is no necessity of giving the public verses, the only merit of which is the source from which they spring."[2]

Timrod began his political commentary with a discussion of "Southern Nationality." Jefferson Davis had not created a nation, he insisted. From the very founding of America, North and South were different, and that dissimilarity of "interests and antagonistic traits, habits, sentiments, opinions and institutions" only increased over the decades. The formation of the Confederacy was the culmination. "It is in these facts that the future philosophic historian will seek the true causes of secession. Abolition and the tariff were little more than the occasions of that moment. If these questions had never arisen, the result, sooner or later, would have been the same." The war might even be seen as a "beneficial evil," he suggested later. "The higher rises the tide of blood, the more impassable the sea, which . . . is destined to flow between us and our foes." So important was separation from the North that "we ought to rejoice at every new barbarity which the enemy perpetrates, every repeated violation of the laws of war which bring down upon him the contempt of the world, and every additional proof which he gives that he is growing more and more reckless in his carnival of crime."

One crime Timrod witnessed was the Federal bombardment of noncombatants in the city of his birth. The cruelty of the enemy is not only "that he has done these things, but that he has done them without the slightest compunction, and has gloated over the supposed sufferings of the defenseless inhabitants." Timrod had only praise for the people of Charleston.

> The streets bustle with trade, the sidewalks are lined with undisturbed pedestrians, children play upon the very outskirts of the fire, sometimes beneath it, and cheerful faces may be seen on every side. There is something affecting, also, in the courage of the women. Most of them heed the shells as little as the sternest veteran. On one occasion, a gentleman passing a house, while the enemy were shelling the town, saw in the piazza a lady in mourning, engaged in the feminine occupation of sewing. A shell whizzed the next moment over the building, and the gentleman paused to witness the demeanor of the fair seamstress. She simply, without rising, followed the flight of the missile with her eyes, heard it explode not a hundred yards distant, and then quietly resumed her work.[3]

In "The Yankee Dissected," on January 23, Timrod explored the utilitarian nature he saw in the enemy.

> The Yankee, the Abolition Yankee, is as *sui generis* as if he belonged to another planet—some sphere where the sun gives just light enough for use, but none for beauty—where the winds only blow and the rivers only run when they have some business to perform. . . . We do not believe that the Yankee ever really beheld a sunset. The light and colors might in some sense have been visible to him, but to the purple islands and crimson archipelagoes of that glorious fairy land in the Western sky, he must be perfectly blind. If for a single second he had ever caught a glimpse of these glories, he would have learned to recognize, faintly at least, the elements of grandeur and sublimity.

Materialism had, in Timrod's view, poisoned their very soul.

> If you wish to cheat him, he will divine your intention in an instant; but you puzzle him painfully if you act towards him in a spirit of unselfish liberality. This is the reason why the Pennsylvanian farmers attributed the leniency of Lee, in his invasion of that State, to a fear of exciting the wrath of the whole Northern people. They were perfectly honest in the misconstruction. How could they detect a motive of which, in their whole lives, they never had, and never could have, the slightest experience?

As if to bolster Timrod's point, it was reported that Federal officers were shipping home the silver, furniture, and artwork stolen from Southern civilians during their raids. "Conceive a number of children brought up in a house," wrote Timrod, "all the most prized ornaments of which are the fruits of the larcenies of the father! How beneficial the influence of such surroundings upon the character! How eminently favorable to the development of those peculiar virtues in which the Yankee especially delights."

Joseph H. Mellichamp, Charleston physician, journeyed to Columbia that winter to purchase supplies. Walking along Richardson (now Main) Street "I heard my name called and shouted almost enthusiastically. I turned and there at some distance was . . . Timrod advancing rapidly to me. 'Doctor—Doctor—Doctor!' His countenance all aglow . . . seemingly with some happy thought, yet he was silent, we two walking together, and I awaiting to hear what I was sure he would tell me. Something seemed bursting almost within him and I knew it had to come out . . . 'Doctor,' he said, 'I have the greatest news to tell you, and about *myself*, too! Do you know I am going to be *married* and I am as happy as I can be!'"

Dr. Mellichamp never forgave himself for his reply. "Well, Mr. Timrod, I am amazed and astonished at what you are going to do—to get married at such a time—when our soldiers are dying daily and soon we know not whether we will have any country at all, and at such a time of gloom and disaster to take a wife."

"I was really in dead earnest, but acted like a damned fool for all that," remembered Mellichamp. "He was the most impressionable fellow I ever met—his whole sweet and jubilant countenance fell—his enthusiasm all gone, and then I saw what I had done in my smartness and folly! We walked on together for perhaps a whole square or more, and not a word passed between us, and I thought I had covered him in such an ice blanket of misery that poor Timrod would never recover himself. But I was mistaken. Love isn't made of that kind of stuff . . . Soon his features brightened . . . and he was indeed himself and I really felt comforted; and after awhile bade him good-bye."[4]

Timrod took a brief break from his editorial duties after but one month on the job. Katie and Henry were married in Columbia on Tuesday, February 16. He was thirty-five years old, she twenty-one. The ceremony was held at noon in Christ Protestant Episcopal Church at the corner of Blanding and Marion streets. Consecrated only four years earlier, the handsome Gothic edifice seated 600 and housed a growing congregation. Rev. J. Maxwell Pringle performed the ceremony.

A formal announcement appeared in the newspaper, but Timrod's journalistic cohorts could not resist comment of their own. "ANOTHER DEFUNCT BACHELOR" was the title of their published notice. "It is with a species of grim satisfaction that we announce in our columns today, another diminution in the ranks of single blessed-dom. Ye 'elbow neighbors' of ye local, and ye pleasant associate of editor—Henry Timrod by name—poet, dreamer, philosopher, and good fellow generally, after suffering for months all the horrors of that worst of 'ills that flesh is heir to'—enlargement of the heart—has at last entered his haven of rest. The nervous, restless, jerky, abstracted individual who was wont to upset our exchange, read papers for hours upside down, write editorials and tear them up, order big fires on hot days and open the doors when it

was cold enough to freeze the legs off a tin kettle—this afflicted cor-
porosity, the Fates be praised, is no more. . . . South Carolina, not
being big enough to hold his swelling soul, he has disappeared into
the profundities of Georgia."[5]

After that short Georgia honeymoon the couple returned to
Columbia and Katie set up housekeeping in their modest, rented
quarters while Timrod went back to work. In April William Gilmore
Simms traveled to Columbia to say good-bye to his son, off to the
front in Virginia. "I saw Timrod," Simms reported to Hayne, "and
was glad to find him in better health and spirits than he has had for
years before. Temperance & employment are doing him good." Timrod's bride may have had something to do with the improvement,
though Simms did not say so. Simms did claim that Timrod had few
responsibilities at the *Carolinian,* but to write "a couple dwarf essays"
each day. "A daily newspaper in a village like Columbia is far different from that of a great commercial city," insisted the former
Charleston editor. Timrod had little time for poetry, but "he is making himself a fine prose writer," and the job "gives him the creature
comforts, & with a young wife, he has need of all he can earn in
these parlous times."[6]

Timrod shared a litany of trifling complaints in his own letters to
Hayne. De Fontaine kept every book sent to the newspaper for review, although Timrod wrote the criticism and therefore felt he had
a right to them. He read few literary journals that might come in the
mail because "Fontaine immediately seizes on them for his wife who
keeps them on file." Timrod promised to publish a new Hayne poem
"as soon as the self-sufficient foreman of the establishment [Selby] . . .
shall decree that it may be admitted without displacing what he con-
siders more important." His new responsibilities had effectively dis-
placed poetry in Timrod's life. To another correspondent he complained of performing nearly all the editorial work, a fact "ignored to
a greater extent than I like."[7]

But there was a lighter side to Timrod's pen. When the promise
of an early spring was shattered in late March by ice and snow, Timrod was amused by the vagaries of Carolina weather. "We had vainly
indulged the hope that old winter had taken up his snowy bed and
walked—decamped for the season—but he is back upon us in all his
frosty ugliness, fiercer than before. The trees in their icy robes look
like ghostly effigies of their former selves; the earth is covered with a

cold, white counterpane; the streets are an omelet of mud and snow." Only weeks later he paused in his work to "gaze through the dingy panes of our office window, at one of the sweetest skies that ever melted into a poet's heart." It was late April.

> After a thousand coquetries, Spring has, at last, flung herself upon the bosom of earth with an abandonment of passion, which seems to argue a willingness to remain there for the rest of the season . . . Trees are not donning their summer clothing, but rushing into it; flowers bud and burst with a suddenness that you are astonished that they don't do it with a snap; and ladies and gentlemen have thrown themselves into a whirl of parties and picnics, in which they go spinning, spinning, as if they had got divinely drunk upon the breath of May.

By August he again sweltered in the heat and humidity of a Deep South summer.

> The poets have said so many pretty things about summer nights, that the sentimental reader will probably accuse us of rank blasphemy when we pronounce them, in an expressive vulgarism, by no means "what they are cracked up to be." The gentle airs, the luscious calms, the golden moons, the silver clouds, are all very well in their way; but when one has to pay for these delights with a thousand other annoyances, one may be pardoned for wishing the sweetest summer night . . . a speedy journey to the underworld.

There were huge, night-flying beetles to battle, and even bats might invade open windows.

> Are your troubles over? Not a whit. After brushing and tucking in the mosquito net, you lay down, in the fond hope of enjoying six or seven hours of undisturbed sleep. Delusive trust! Vain hallucination! Just as the lids of the mind are about closing. . . . you hear, at a little distance above you, a fine, sharp sound, like that produced by a low wind among reeds; and presently, with the unerring aim of an eagle, down into the very orifice of your ear, as if he would penetrate the secret crypts of your brain, swoops the deadliest enemy that a devotee of Morpheus has ever to encounter—a hungry mosquito!. . . . Slap! Slap! Your hand burns, your fingers tingle with the violence of the concussion. Nothing is hurt but yourself. The nimble foe escapes every blow in the dark. At every pause, you hear the small horn of your antagonist sounding like an elfin bugle in defiance.[8]

From the beginning of the war the editorial policy of Rhett's Charleston *Mercury* had been to blame the Davis administration for every setback and undermine the president's leadership with a constant chorus of complaint. Not Timrod's *Carolinian.*

> One purpose alone has actuated us in the conduct of this journal. It is to contribute all that journalists can contribute to the achievement of the complete, unqualified, and lasting independence of the Confederate States. In comparison with that object, everything else that makes life precious is, to us, a matter of secondary consideration, for the simple reason that, upon the attainment of that object, the permanent preservation of everything that makes life precious, absolutely depends.

He was not unmindful of complaints that the Confederate government had enlarged its powers. With the coming of peace

> it will be necessary that we should examine the ship of state, and see how far it has been damaged by the breakers over which it has passed. We shall then note exactly where the General Government has been forced by the exigencies of the war to encroach upon the sovereignty of the States ... and to re-affirm, with every solemn formality, all the guarantees of the Constitution, and all the principles of conservative Republicanism.[9]

Timrod was quick to editorially defend Southern Jews and condemn any tendency "to treat them scornfully." He reminded fellow Confederates that "when we count the roll of the living and dead who are and have been in the front ranks of our armies, it will be found that the Jew has given his life and services as freely to the country, in proportion to population, as any other class of the community."[10]

In July Timrod reflected on the fact that Independence Day had come to be largely ignored in the South. He was certainly glad to be rid of yesterday's "patriotic sentimentality" and "turgid rhetoric." Still,

> we have no inclination to deprive that day of its just honors on which was, for the first time, effectively and solemnly enunciated, "the right of the people to alter and abolish a form of Government, deriving its just powers from the consent of the governed." This is the principle for which we are even now contending, and which we have never violated; and, therefore, whatever associations are connected with that

mid-summer day in the year of our Lord 1776, ought to be peculiarly and perpetually cherished by the citizens and citizen-soldiers of these Confederate States. When the time and our means permit, we shall be glad to see renewed, with every return of the occasion, the bonfires and rejoicings with which it used to be celebrated, and we shall read, with hardly less pleasure than in the season of our boyhood, the familiar but ever fresh truths appropriate to the day written by the art of the pyrotechnist in letters of emerald and crimson against the dusk evening sky.

"The nation which forgets its martyred dead," Timrod wrote just days later, "can do no honor to its living heroes." His thoughts were on the tens of thousands who had already perished in the cause of Southern independence.

Perhaps almost as many sleep beneath the sod as are now marching above to defend it. We have laid a whole army in the earth. If we are just, we will not regard that army as altogether lost to us, or its services as altogether finished. . . . Out of myriads of graves, its blood cries unto God and the nations in our behalf; the plants which wrap their roots around the bones of its heroes whisper, with all their leaves, lessons of solemn self-sacrifice, and make the air heavy as with the fragrance of noble deeds; and in the hour of battle, when to the stirred soul and excited fancy metaphor becomes fact, and the cherished memories of the heart are ready to take bodily shape, the ghosts of its shadowy columns seem to float above our standards, and fight once more upon our side! If there be any truth in moral and spiritual influences, the might of that dead army remains with us yet!

To Timrod, it was not possible that even a single one of these men died in vain.

The family which mourns his loss as an irremediable grief, finds that loss, as the slow moon rolls on, becoming an august recollection, to which it recurs with pride, and from which its children receive their first lessons in the stern duties of life. And what each fallen patriot is to a family, the glorious body of martyrs will be to the country at large. Their deeds and their fate transmuted into history and poetry, "far on in summers that we shall not see," will be an entire national education in themselves.[11]

In summer Timrod was ill, but soon rebounded. He visited Simms at his "Woodlands" plantation home. In August Simms was in Columbia to ask Timrod's help. Though it never came to fruition, Simms planned to edit a volume of Mother Goose rhymes for Southern children. "I am making it as original as possible," he wrote Hayne, "that is to say, adapting it to Southern life, peculiarities, characteristics, &c. If you have ever manufactured any doggrel rhymes for your little boy, or can *descend* to the effort, send me some. [John Dickson] Bruns has done so, & sent me some very clever ones . . ." The only pay he could promise was a copy of the book when published. Decades earlier Timrod's father had contrived with friends a practical joke around Simms' purported editing of "Jack the Giant Killer," but by now the irony was lost on him. He would ask Timrod, Simms told Hayne, to contribute to his collection of nursery rhymes "in anticipation of the boy forthcoming."[12]

It was probably in early summer that Katie told her husband that she was expecting a child. Timrod could only be thrilled with the news. Five months into the pregnancy, on August 25, he reported to Hayne that Katie "is threatened with a miscarriage, and though comparatively better this morning than she has been for the last two or three days, there is still some uncertainty about the event."[13]

Katie recovered and the danger to the unborn baby passed. But little more than a week later, on September 5, her brother George Goodwin died, after "a long and weary illness," according to the newspaper notice. Just forty-four years old, never more than a marginal success in business, he was said to have yet been a generous man. "I well remember the fearful hours when he was taken from me," Emily said later. "Hope then seemed to die out of my existence, and a horror of darkness and despair seemed to close around me."[14]

Only days before Goodwin's death the telegraph brought the South disheartening news. Atlanta had fallen to Union general William Tecumseh Sherman after his relentless campaign through northern Georgia. Sherman soon began his devastating "March to the Sea" after burning Atlanta. "The time is at hand when every man should be up and doing," wrote Timrod. "The enemy is in the heart of Georgia, and every hour is approaching nearer to the borders of our State. If unopposed, he may reach Augusta; Charleston may be threatened; Columbia will be in danger—great danger. . . . The situation is a grave one. Are we preparing for it?" Even if Sherman's army never reached central South Carolina, Timrod warned that Union raiding parties might. He urged immediate action.

If Columbia is to be defended, it is high time we should be about it. If the Confederate authorities are too busy, let the matter be taken in hand by the State. Give us works, behind which to fight, redoubts on our roads; and organization to our people. There are brigades of men in this city who can do battle for one day at least, and every one who can hold a musket, should have his place.

Union troops looted and torched everything they could lay their hands on in a path sixty miles wide through Georgia. "We have Sherman's word that it is his wish to conduct the war on civilized principles," mocked Timrod.

It will be our fault, he insinuates, if he does not. . . . The inhabitants of an invaded district have no right to annoy an invading army in any way. To plant a single obstacle in the path of the beneficent power which comes to take care of their property and to relieve them of the "weight of too much liberty," is a crime justly provocative of the bitterest retaliation.

On December 21 Savannah fell to Sherman's 62,000-man army. There remained but a comparative handful of Confederates to defend South Carolina. In the spirit of John Brown, Sherman's men swore to show no mercy on those they blamed for the war.

The *Carolinian* backed President Davis' eleventh-hour plan to enlist blacks, though thousands already served the Confederate army in a support role. Timrod remembered when General John Bell Hood went in search of 3,000 teamsters. Plantation owners assembled their work forces, asked for volunteers, and more stepped forward than were needed. Black combat troops could serve their country as well, thought Timrod. "We want help. We want laboring men and fighting men, and if proper measures be adopted, we believe that twenty thousand [slaves] may be induced to volunteer within ninety days. The breeze need only be started to become a whirlwind."[15]

Timrod's newspaper published on November 6 his short "Hymn Sung At a Sacred Concert at Columbia, S. C.," the only poem he had written in nearly a year. His theme of dependence on God echoed an earlier editorial.

Let the infidel or the mocker prate as he may about the Lord being "on the side of the strongest battalions." Our whole history has been a palpable denial of the imperious assertion. . . . Let us, then, all look reverently once more to that Supreme Being whose testimony written in our behalf, and whose love entwined with our destiny, has so often proved Him to be our "very present help in time of need."

Timrod quoted one Charleston lady's proclamation of the ancient Hebrew motto: Jehovah–Nissi—the Lord is our banner. "How suitable to be inscribed on the heart and standard of a people who are defending their homes and altars! How appropriate for those who are fighting, not to acquire the possessions of others, but to defend all that it is their duty to love and protect!" "Let Jehovah–Nissi be ever in our heart," Timrod concluded, "and Jehovah–Jira—the Lord will provide."[16]

On Christmas Eve Henry and Katie were blessed with the birth of a son. Named William Henry Timrod after his grandfather, the parents would call him simply "Willie." Soon Hayne received a letter he described as "bubbling over with pride and delight." The new father reported to his friend that finally "we stand upon the same height of paternity—quite a celestial elevation to me! If you could only see my boy! Everybody wonders at him! He is so transparently fair; so ethereal!"[17]

10

"O saddest child of Time"

In January of 1865 Captain William A. Courtenay of the Confederate Quartermaster Department awaited the arrival of his train at the station in Branchville, Orangeburg District. There he ran into Timrod, perhaps gathering facts on the military situation for his newspaper. Courtenay was a little younger than his friend, and had also grown up in Charleston, working in a bookstore there. The two talked for hours. "He was then in feeble health, depressed in spirits," remembered Courtenay. The conversation inevitably turned to their common love of poetry. "I recall his plaintive regret at the apparently hopeless task of collecting and publishing his poems. He spoke of his repeated disappointment in life, but kept dwelling upon the non-publication of his literary works."

"Harry, we are all in a great deal of trouble," said Courtenay, "the future is very uncertain, and promises may be difficult to fulfill, but if my life is spared, and I can accomplish your wish, I promise you I will do it."

"Will you?" said Timrod, as he jumped to his feet and grabbed Courtenay's hands. "Will you?"

"Yes," replied Courtenay, "I will certainly do it if I can."[1]

The trouble Courtenay spoke of was not long in coming. On February first Sherman ordered his troops across the Savannah River. The invasion of South Carolina had begun, and every man in that army knew what was expected of him. Homes, farms, whole towns and villages—all were plundered and burned. "In South Carolina there was no restraint whatsoever in pillaging and foraging," wrote a soldier from Michigan. "Men were allowed to do as they liked, *burn and destroy.*" The destruction was carried out, said an Illinois major, "not under orders, but in spite of orders." "We marched with thousands of columns of smoke marking the line of each corps," remembered one Union division commander. "The sights at times, as seen from elevated grounds, were often terribly sublime."

As the invaders neared Columbia, hopelessly outnumbered Confederates burned bridges over the rivers that were the Capital's only natural defensive barriers. A fearful De Fontaine evacuated most of his paper's hoard of newsprint and supplies to the upper part of the state. On the cold morning of February 16—the Timrods' first wedding anniversary—Sherman's artillery began lobbing shells into the heart of the city. "Mr. Timrod and myself remained here," remembered Selby, "and issued a 'thumb sheet' two or three times a day (not a pleasant occupation with shells dropping in the neighborhood of the building)—having retained the small amount of printing material necessary."[2]

When Southern soldiers withdrew, Mayor Thomas Jefferson Goodwyn surrendered his city and was promised protection by the conquering Federals. But that very night fires set by blue-clad incendiaries broke out all over town. Suburban homes were targeted as well. Citizens were robbed at gunpoint on the streets. "As one whose vigorous, patriotic editorials had made him obnoxious to Federal vengeance," said Hayne, "Timrod was forced, while this foreign army occupied the town, to remain concealed." Three days later Sherman's troops continued their northward march. Timrod, said Hayne, "rejoined his anxious 'womankind,' to behold, in common with thousands of others, such a scene of desolation as mortal eyes have seldom dwelt upon." The capitol gone, the unfinished new State House pockmarked by cannon fire, much of the rest of Columbia—including the main business district—was in smoldering ruins. The *South Carolinian* office was destroyed. Even Christ Church was in ashes. Many of the homeless camped in city parks with little shelter against February's cold. Timrod, Katie, and Willie moved in with Emily Goodwin and her children and extended family. Thankfully, the home she rented had escaped the flames.

With Sherman's departure what remained of Columbia returned to Confederate control. There would be more battles and skirmishes—additional dead and wounded—before Lee was forced to surrender his Army of Northern Virginia on April 12. Within weeks other Confederate commands also laid down their arms. President Davis was soon a prisoner. On May 25 a contingent of Federal troops marched to Columbia, arrested the governor, and garrisoned the city.[3]

His business gone, money worthless, without work or income, Timrod and his family struggled for survival. They sold possessions to buy food. Thinking he might find employment in the North, on July 10 Timrod wrote to Richard H. Stoddard, the New York critic who had praised his poetry years earlier. He spoke frankly. In the war "I was a secessionist in opinion, though the state of my health precluded my bearing arms. But the logic of events has made me once more a citizen of the United States; I begin to see (darkly) behind that *Divine* political economy which has ended in the extinction of slavery and the preservation of the Union; and I am prepared to discharge in good faith the obligations which I assumed upon taking the oath. More I need not say; you are a poet of a high order, you must possess that universality of mind which will not permit you to regard with the narrow prejudices of the mere politician those who differ with you in creed." Timrod confessed to having been reduced "to the most abject poverty." He thought of again teaching, "but can get no pupils, as nobody is rich enough to pay tuition fees. All alike are ruined . . . Those who have lately visited us from your section have been struck aghast. You will not wonder, therefore, that I should desire to get away. I have a family to support, and here they must starve. With what reception would a Southerner meet in New York? Could I hope to get employment there in any capacity whatever? Hack writer of a newspaper, editor of the poet's corner of some third-rate journal, grocer's clerk—nothing would come amiss to me that would put bread into the mouths and a roof over the heads of those whom I love best in the whole world."[4]

Stoddard was moved by Timrod's plight. He did not encourage him to relocate, but did ask at least one literary friend to contact Timrod about publishing some of his poems. "He's a true poet, the best, I conceive, that the South has yet produced."[5] Late that summer Timrod wrote Stoddard his thanks, enclosing several previously published poems he thought might be acceptable to a Northern audience. He had good news to report. "You will be glad to hear that my prospects are somewhat better than when I wrote you two months ago. I expect ere long to be associated in the editorial department of a daily paper about to be established either here [Columbia] or at Charleston. Once in harness, I need not tell you that I shall not have much time to contribute either in prose or verse to the pages of a magazine." He closed with the comment that he wrote with difficulty, "being sick myself and in the same room with my sick babe."

There was a postscript, dated October first. "This letter has been lying on my desk for three weeks. A thousand anxieties have conspired to make me neglect it. A sister and my only child are now lying exceedingly ill under my roof."[6]

Two days later Edith Caroline Timrod Cotchett, wife of Ainsley H. Cotchett, was dead. Thirty-two years old, she was the youngest of Timrod's sisters and may have died as the result of complications from childbirth. It is known that a baby, given the name Edith Emily, was born on October first and soon adopted by Emily Goodwin. The little girl would herself live but seven months.[7]

The newspaper job referred to by Timrod was again with the *Daily South Carolinian*. De Fontaine told him the paper would begin publishing in Charleston, and initially "promised that I should have my old interest as a partner." Timrod went on to tell Hayne, now living in Georgia, that his editor treated him as an employee, offering but $15 per week. Timrod halfheartedly accepted, submitting a little material through the mail despite his ill health. Associate editor William Gilmore Simms complained that "De Fontaine is absent most of the time, and Timrod does not contribute a line for weeks together." Timrod received little or no pay, but could not fault De Fontaine, as the *Carolinian* was "languishing and will die" under that city's long-established newspaper competition. "He made a grave mistake in carrying his paper to Charleston," concluded Timrod.[8]

Another reason Timrod was unable to contribute more was continued worry over his sick child. And on October 9—less than a week after Edith's death—Rebecca Adeline Timrod died. Firstborn of William Henry and Thyrza Timrod's children, and crippled from birth, she never married. Timrod's seventy-year-old mother had lost two children in six days.

Then, on the morning of Wednesday, October 23, little Willie succumbed. He was under ten months old. The cause of his death is not known. The funeral was held at 10 o'clock the following morning at Trinity, Columbia's surviving Episcopal Church. "In that little grave, a large portion of the father's heart was buried," wrote Hayne. "The poet was never quite his old self again."[9]

Months later Timrod was able to write two poems about Willie and the pain he and Katie felt in losing him. "Our Willie" tells of joy the Christmas he was born, and how that day is now spent mourning beside his grave. Timrod lovingly described their infant.

> That wandering hand which seemed to reach
>   At angel finger-tips,
> And that murmur like a mystic speech
>   Upon the rosy lips,
> That something in the serious face
> Holier than even its infant grace,
> And that rapt gaze on empty space,

A glimpse of their anguish—and even anger—is seen in the middle stanzas of "A Mother's Wail."

> My babe! my babe! my own and only babe!
> Where art thou now? If somewhere in the sky
> An angel hold thee in his radiant arms,
> I challenge him to clasp thy tender form
> With half the fervor of a mother's love!
>
> Forgive me, Lord! forgive my reckless grief!
> Forgive me that this rebel, selfish heart
> Would almost make me jealous for my child,
> Though thy own lap enthroned him. Lord thou hast
> So many such! I have—ah! had but one!
>
> O yet once more, my babe, to hear thy cry!
> O yet once more, my babe, to see thy smile!
> O yet once more to feel against my breast
> Those cool, soft hands, that warm, wet, eager mouth,
> With the sweet sharpness of its budding pearls!
>
> But it must never, never more be mine
> To mark the growing meaning in thine eyes,
> To watch thy soul unfolding leaf by leaf,
> Or catch, with ever fresh surprise and joy,
> Thy dawning recognition of the world.[10]

Soon thereafter Timrod met a sympathetic friend, William J. Rivers, walking in Columbia. A professor at South Carolina College, Rivers had taught young Timrod in Charleston years before. "I can recall Timrod as he stood," said Rivers, "agitated by his feelings in a quiet spot of a street to read to me what he had just composed, a wail for the death of his little son."[11]

"You ask me to tell you my story of the last year," wrote Timrod to Hayne. "I can embody it all in a few words—beggary, starvation, death, bitter grief, utter want of hope. But I'll be a little more particular, that you may learn where I stand. . . . Both my sister [Emily] and myself are completely impoverished. We have lived for a long period, and are still living, on the gradual sale, of furniture and plate. We have eaten two silver pitchers, one or two dozen forks, several sofas innumerable chairs, and a bedstead." Not only was there no market for his poetry, he had no desire to write. Indeed, "I feel perfectly indifferent to the fate of what I have written. I would consign ever[y] line I ever wrote to eternal oblivion for one-hundred dollars in hand."[12]

The year 1865 had seen the downfall of Timrod's country, the death of two sisters, and of his baby boy. He had lost his home and his business in the burning of Columbia. Yet he retained a glimmer of hope. "1866: Addressed to the Old Year" appeared on the first page of the *South Carolinian* on New Year's Eve, December 31, 1865.

> ART thou not glad to close
>   Thy wearied eyes, O saddest child of Time,
>   Eyes which have looked on every mortal crime,
> And swept the piteous round of mortal woes?
>
> In dark Plutonian caves,
>   Beneath the lowest deep, go, hide thy head;
>   Or earth thee where the blood that thou hast shed
> May trickle on thee from thy countless graves!
>
> Take with thee all thy gloom
>   And guilt, and all our griefs, save what the breast
>   Without a wrong to some dear shadowy guest,
> May not surrender even to the tomb.

No tear shall weep thy fall,
>When, as the midnight bell doth toll thy fate,
>Another lifts the sceptre of thy state,
And sits a monarch in thine ancient hall.

. . . .

Beneath his gentle hand
>They hope to see no meadow, vale, or hill
>Stained with a deeper red than roses spill,
When some too boisterous zephyr sweeps the land.

A time of peaceful prayer,
>Of law, love, labor, honest loss and gain—
>These are the visions of the coming reign
Now floating to them on this wintry air.[13]

De Fontaine planned to return his newspaper to Columbia from Charleston. Timrod still wrote articles for it irregularly. In "Spring's Lessons" he hailed the coming of the season that might truly reconstruct the South, bringing "forgetfulness of the past, effort in the present, and trust in the future!" But he was not about to forget Confederate heroism. Timrod relished the idea of retrieving relics from the wreck of the *C. S. S. Alabama,* resting underwater off the coast of Cherbourg, France. "For what a wonderful history was hers! A single ship matched against one of the mightiest navies of the world . . ."[14]

Rails linking Columbia to the coast, wrecked by Sherman, had finally been replaced. "I can tell you nothing about Charleston," Timrod told Hayne. "I ran down there in February—and spent three days there; but my eyes were blind to every thing and every body but a few old friends. I dined with Bruns, had a night of it at Henry Raimonds, and went to see the lions in the circus." John Dickson Bruns was an old friend, and even Katie professed "to stand very much in awe of him." Raimond's may have been a tavern. A traveling circus, with a lion tamer, performed on Citadel Square—just a few blocks from Timrod's birthplace on King Street. He was glad to have "a free ticket on the railroad—almost the only advantage I have yet derived from my connection with the Carolinian." He went again to Charleston on March 31 to see Bruns off on a voyage to study medicine in London.[15]

In late March the Timrods and Goodwins moved to a rented house on Lady Street in Columbia that they shared with two other families. "Your mother occupies the front room upstairs," he wrote to niece Edith, "from which she can see down the whole street, which is lined with three rows of trees. I and Katie look from the back windows on the suburbs of the town and enough of the country to give us quite a rural feeling."[16]

Timrod worked infrequently for the *Carolinian*. Simms again complained. "Mr. De Fontaine still lingers at the North, doing, Heaven knows what, and delaying heaven knows why. . . . Mr. Timrod has done nothing to assist me for five weeks." Both Timrod and Katie had been ill most of the month. "Coarse food, and not enough of *that*, retard my convalescence," he told Hayne. "I get through George Bryan an invitation from [publisher C. Benjamin Richardson] to go to New York and be his guest. He talks of publishing selections from my poems richly illustrated . . ."[17] Wisely, this time Timrod did not get his hopes up. Like the Vizetelly project, nothing came of it.

Another, more practical offer came to Timrod from Bryan. In April the fifty-five-year-old lawyer and friend of the late Petigru was appointed Federal District Court judge. He was arguably the one living jurist in South Carolina with "unionist" credentials, and had in his youth been a friend of William Henry Timrod. The new judge appointed Daniel Horlbeck clerk, and Henry Timrod assistant clerk. Timrod worked, at least briefly, for the United States judiciary; probably when Judge Bryan's court was in session in Columbia.[18]

Timrod told Hayne about a request he had received from a committee of ladies in Richmond. "It was, to write within a fortnight, a poem on the history of 'Fort Sumter,' . . . long enough to fill *eighty printed octavo pages*, or,—it was obligingly qualified—less!! Need I say that I respectfully declined to undertake the task?"[19]

He accepted a more modest appeal from Charleston. The Ladies' Association to Commemorate the Confederate Dead asked Timrod, and two others, to write poems for a memorial observance they planned for Saturday, June 16, 1866, at Magnolia Cemetery. It was perhaps the first such effort in Charleston since the end of the war, and coincided with the fourth anniversary of the Battle of Secessionville. Magnolia Cemetery was then the resting place of more than 600 Confederates. On the morning of the sixteenth, wagons proceeded through the streets of the city collecting floral decorations and evergreens for transport to the cemetery. Stores closed before noon. Despite a heavy rain, thousands boarded carriages, wagons, omnibuses, and railroad cars for the four-mile trip up the peninsula. "A colored man who had lost a limb fighting for the Confederate cause at the battle of Secessionville," wrote a reporter from the *Courier,* "was also present, watching with interest and assisting in the arrangements and decorations of the graves." By five o'clock the skies cleared and the program began around the stage that had been erected. Between speakers, the choir—under the direction of Thomas P. O'Neale and accompanied by a melodeon—sang the poems.

Timrod's was especially well-received. The *Courier* printed it in their Monday edition, calling the poem "beautiful and soul-stirring." An "amended copy" was reprinted five weeks later "by request."

The best known of Henry Timrod's works, most critics consider it his finest.

Ode

Sung on the Occasion of Decorating the Graves
of the Confederate Dead, at Magnolia Cemetery,
Charleston, S. C., 1866

Sleep sweetly in your humble graves,
    Sleep, martyrs of a fallen cause!—
Though yet no marble column craves
    The pilgrim here to pause.

In seeds of laurels in the earth,
    The garlands of your fame are sown;
And, somewhere, waiting for its birth,
    The shaft is in the stone.

Meanwhile, your sisters for the years
    Which hold in trust your storied tombs,
Bring all they now can give you—tears,
    And these memorial blooms.

Small tributes, but your shades will smile
    As proudly on these wreaths to-day,

As when some cannon-moulded pile
　　Shall overlook this Bay.

Stoop, angels, hither from the skies!
　　There is no holier spot of ground,
Than where defeated valor lies
　　By mourning beauty crowned.[20]

11

"Love is sweeter than rest"

Timrod, according to Simms, "is one of the best of the Southern poets, refined & highly polished, with a fine meditative tone, & a pure and graceful fancy." He was also one of those "helpless because of their endowment, in a world which knows not its uses, and again helpless, in his case, by reason & temperament." Simms described Timrod in October 1866 to Hayne as "the very prince of Dolefuls, and swallowed up in distresses. He now contemplates separation from his wife, that she may go forth as a governess, and he as a tutor, in private families. He can earn nothing where he is—has not a dollar—goes to bed hungry every night—, and suffers from bad health. It is the mortifying thing to all of us, that *none of us* can help him."[1] After receiving Simms' report, Hayne recorded in his diary, "My God! that the best poet of the South should be left to such a Fate." The contemplated family separation never came to pass as there was little demand for governesses or tutors.

Timrod could wear a brighter countenance on occasion. A visiting Northern editor met him about this time "amidst the ruins of the once beautiful city of Columbia. We were struck at once with the beauty of his character. He seemed to us the impersonation of a gentleness that won our heart at the first interview. Although reticent on other topics, we found him ready to communicate on the prospects of Southern literature."[2]

Emily Goodwin arranged employment for her daughters through Sophie Sosnowski Schaller in Athens, Georgia. At Sophie's urging, Emily thought of moving there herself. Madame Sosnowski's school for girls had reopened in Athens and begun to prosper. "I had hoped then that Henry would have been able to provide for himself

and Kate," Emily wrote to Sophie. "But poor fellow! in every applica-
tion he has made, he has been equally unfortunate, and were I to accept the situation you offer I should have to turn him and Katie into
the street. This I could not do. So we shall have to battle it together
for awhile longer." Sophie was the wife of Colonel Frank Schaller
and mother of a young daughter. "My heart aches for Katie T. and
wish that she and Mr. T. had a bright prospect before them," replied
Sophie.[3]

Timrod and his sister thought for a time of operating their own
girls' school. A little advertisement appeared in the Columbia
Phoenix, probably paid for by occasional prose contributions Timrod
made to Selby's new paper. The notice solicited students to be
taught at Emily's home by her and her brother. Classes would begin
in October, "providing a certain number of pupils can be obtained
by that time."[4] As with his hopes to return to tutoring, the poverty of
his fellow countrymen doomed this idea as well.

Civil government had been restored to South Carolina—in name
if not in fact—by the presidential appointment of a "provisional governor" in mid-1865. The state's first postwar voting for that office
took place in November. James L. Orr was elected. Conservative,
white South Carolinians tried to hold on to the reins of state government, though ever mindful of the new political realities. President
Andrew Johnson pursued a moderate policy toward the defeated
South. Radicals in Congress pushed their own plan for "Reconstruction"—a scheme that would sweep fellow Republicans into power
with the votes of newly enfranchised ex-slaves.

Timrod found that he still had friends with the influence to offer
some assistance. "Yes, I have had a sad and hard struggle of it for the
past six months," he wrote to Hayne on November 19, 1866, "but just
as I was about to despair of help from God or man, I received from
Governor Orr a temporary appointment as an assistant or rather
clerk." The job came by way of the governor's overworked secretary,
James S. Simons, who was given permission to hire a helper. It was
no permanent solution to Timrod's financial problems. "It ensures
me, however, of a month's supply of bread and bacon—that de-
voured, I will trust in God that something else may turn up." His day
was ten hours long, from 9 A.M. to 7 P.M. On two occasions during
the legislative session he labored all day and all night. Timrod's desk
was lighted during daylight hours by a window on the west side of

the house on Bull Street that served as the governor's office. Though originally hired for a single month, he would be called back to part-time work as needed. Orr once dictated the main points he wanted to make in an address to the General Assembly, leaving it to Timrod to write the speech. One who witnessed Timrod's efforts saw how sick he was. "In spite of this he was faithful and diligent in the discharge of his duties."[5]

Hayne invited his friend to visit him in Georgia. Timrod regretted that "I must stay here to scratch for corn." Hayne had a young son named Willie. "You say nothing about Mrs Hayne and Willie," Timrod scolded in his letter, "—ah! how ineffably dear that name has become to me now! He was the sweetest child! But everybody thought him too ethereal to live, even when he seemed in most perfect health." Timrod asked Hayne to remember him to his wife, "and to the namesake of my boy."[6]

Around Christmas Timrod was visited by a Methodist minister bearing a gift of money from Wade Hampton. Before the war one of the South's wealthiest men, Hampton had lost much of his property, his home, a son, and a brother in that conflict. He had commanded Lee's cavalry corps and risen to the rank of lieutenant general. A vestryman at Trinity Church, Hampton was well acquainted with Timrod and his family's needs. There are several versions of how the gift was given. In each a proud Timrod is at first reluctant to accept charity, but relents when the donor persists. With much emotion a grateful Timrod credits God with sending the aid. Other friends contributed over the following months. "I was fortunate enough to procure for him $115," said Simms, "which is eked out to him . . . at $20 per week."[7]

Simms put forth a considerable effort to raise the sum for his friend, but doled out the money, he said, because Timrod "always suffers from the sin of impecuniosity." One day Simms called, but found only Katie and Emily at home. "He entertained them by enlarging upon the readiness with which I yield to *mere lassitude*," wrote Timrod. "He said that once in Charleston he had called on me, and found me lying on my back, slightly indisposed, and reading a 'yellow covered novel.'" Timrod remembered the incident. He had truly been sick, he said, and was in fact reading Shakespeare. "I have not read ten novels in as many years, and I never read trash, not even Mr Simms." Simms had not allowed Katie or Emily to utter a word in

Timrod's defense. "He is lazy, Timrod was always lazy," insisted Simms. "Save me from such a friend," concluded Timrod.[8]

In late January 1867 the Timrods and Goodwins again moved—only a block and a half—to a smaller, more affordable home. They had shared a house with Dr. Robert W. Gibbes' family. "We regretted the separation very much as the two families had become very much attached," Emily wrote to Sophie Schaller. The Goodwins and Timrods now lived next door to Peter Shand, rector of Trinity Church; Emily was glad "that we shall have pleasant neighbors."[9]

During the winter Timrod and Katie were ill. But at the end of March they had improved and he thought again of journeying north in search of employment. Hayne could provide introductions to the literary critic Edwin P. Whipple and publisher James T. Fields, both in Boston. "But alas! where shall I get the golden or paper wings to waft me thither," he asked Hayne. "Yet I shall need but little, and shall endeavor to raise it . . . I can't set out, however, before the middle of May—as I could not stand a Northern climate at an earlier season."[10] He thought too of visiting John R. Thompson in New York. Timrod sent Thompson a few poems, but was unable to provide the requested likeness of himself for Thompson's proposed edition of Southern war poems. "The truth is," confessed Timrod, "I am so poor at present as to put even the petty cost of a photograph utterly beyond my means." Timrod's "A Mother's Wail" moved Thompson. "When I read his poems," he told Hayne, "I feel so deep a sense of utter inferiority that I almost vow I will never write another line." A month later Timrod was finally able to forward a photographic image to Thompson, " a contribution of Messrs Wearn & Hicks [Hix], Artists of Columbia."[11]

"Your cordial invitation to your homestead," Timrod wrote Hayne in mid-April, "I mean as soon as possible, to answer in person. The doctor has long advised me to change my air for a little while . . ." Hayne was living with his wife, son, and mother at "Copse Hill," the home he described as a "Small white-washed cottage rudely built of unseasoned lumber and clapboards of pine." On eighteen wooded acres, sixteen miles from Augusta on the Georgia Railroad, he spent his days there writing, taking walks, cutting wood, and hunting. "I left the world, that is to say,—Society,—to take up my abode in the wilderness; literally, the wilderness," he wrote of his secluded retreat. Rather than head north in search of work Timrod determined to visit his old friend. He hoped to secure free railroad tickets, but promised to come regardless.[12]

Timrod arrived at "Copse Hill" during the second week in May and stayed the remainder of the month. "He found me with my family," remembered Hayne, "established in a crazy wooden shanty, dignified as a cottage. . . . and in the enthusiasm of the poet's welcome we strove to make amends for the general poverty of his accommodations, and a very perceptible coarseness of the *cuisine*." Hayne discovered that Timrod simply enjoyed the solitude of the country and the warm spring sunshine. He loved to rest on a bed of pine needles as he listened to the wind in the tree tops. Timrod was touched by kindnesses shown him by Hayne's wife and mother. "His nature was so pure—so childlike—so unfitted for this hard life," said Mrs. Paul Hayne. In Willie, Timrod seemed to embrace the image of his own son.

Upon returning to Columbia Timrod again complained of pain in his chest and a persistent cough. "I have that feeling which . . . [it is said] precedes death, and makes it easy," he confided in a July letter to Hayne, "a feeling as if the ties that bind me to earth are gradually loosening, and as if I could see them broken altogether without much regret. Don't think, however, that I am 'giving up.' I shall make a brave struggle for life."[13]

Sad news came that month from Athens. Sophie Sosnowski Schaller died unexpectedly. "For such a loss as you have sustained there is indeed no consolation in this world," Timrod wrote to Frank Schaller. "Your wife was a woman of such uncommon beauty of character, that you seem to me to have parted with the very angel of your life!" For Sophie to die at the age of thirty was something never contemplated by the author of "Two Portraits." Timrod made reference to Schaller's Christian faith. "What an exquisite though solemn happiness it must be to you in your agony, to think that at the end of that long dark path which you will henceforth travel almost alone, a blessed saint waits to welcome you to your rest!" He closed with a promise to try to visit him in Athens.

The next day Katie Timrod penned a letter of condolence to Sophie's sister Kallie that contained as much anger as it did comfort. "I am not a Christian, and I cannot draw consolation from the thought that God is love. I can only think of the desolate mother; the husband whose life is forever darkened, and of the brother and sister who have lost in their dead sister their dearest household idol. I can only think of the little motherless ones . . ."[14]

There was one offer of employment made to Timrod that summer. It was proposed, apparently by an associate of Julian Selby, that a weekly paper be launched in Charleston with Timrod as editor. He would be paid $10 per week. Timrod reluctantly accepted, if he would be permitted to work from his Columbia home. The owner of this projected journal was woefully short of capital. He directed Timrod to ask writer Clara Dargan if she would be willing to submit a serial story, beginning with the premiere issue on October 1. "His offer is to pay you providing his paper prove a success, and your story contribute to that success!" Embarrassed by having to convey such an offer, Timrod invited Dargan to propose her own terms, if interested, and to write to him at Paul Hayne's Georgia address. He was about to make another visit.[15]

Timrod departed Columbia by rail on Thursday, August 8, and spent three weeks at "Copse Hill." The two poets whiled away their time daydreaming as if they were boys again. "We would rest on the hillsides," said Hayne, "in the swaying golden shadows, watching together the Titanic masses of snow-white clouds which floated slowly and vaguely through the sky, suggesting . . . flotillas of icebergs upon Artic seas." Timrod enjoyed sunsets. In the evenings he read aloud from volumes of verse he found on Hayne's bookshelves. "Hayne has plenty of new books," Timrod wrote his sister. "It is hard to tell which to begin first. I distract [myself] by insane attempts to read all of them." In a conversation one evening just before he left to come home Timrod spoke of literary figures who had reached advanced ages.

"I hav'nt the slightest desire, Paul, to be an octogenarian, far less a centenarian . . . but I *do* hope that I may be spared until I am *fifty* or fifty-five."

"About Shakespeare's age," Hayne replied.

"Oh!" smiled Timrod, "I was not thinking of *that*; but I'm sure that after fifty-five I would begin to wither, mind and body, and one hates the idea of a mummy, intellectual or physical."

Without the money to buy a ticket to Athens—and probably not wanting to leave "Copse Hill" before he had to—Timrod abandoned thoughts of visiting niece Edith Goodwin and the Schallers. On his way to the Augusta station to take the train to Columbia he was handed an envelope from the post office. It contained a money order for $6, payment for a sonnet he had sent *Southern Opinion*. The royalty was most welcome. "I did not come home a moment too soon," he told Hayne. "I found [my family] without money or provisions."[16]

"You will be surprised and pained to hear that I have had a severe hemorrhage of the lungs," Timrod wrote to Hayne less than two weeks after his return. It may have begun while he met with friends Hugh Thompson and William Talley on Friday evening, September 13. Timrod was said to have had his proof sheets with him, and some pages became stained with his blood. "It came upon me without a moments warning . . ." Two days later there was another episode. "It occurred in the street—the blood came in jets from my mouth—you might have traced me home in crimson," he wrote the next day. "It is an awkward time for me to be sick—we are wholly destitute of funds & almost of food. But God will provide. I have learned to trust in him."[17]

Days earlier he had written a sonnet as an obituary for Harris Simons, a Charleston friend recently deceased. It was the last poem Timrod would write.[18]

Emily declined, on her brother's behalf, the editorship of the proposed Charleston weekly. Only a week after that first episode of bleeding she reported to Hayne in her own hand. "Yesterday morning I was called hurriedly to his room, a much more violent hemorrhage than any of the preceding ones having occurred. The blood was pouring from his mouth with such violence as to threaten astrangulation." She was terrified. Katie screamed. Timrod's mother wrung her hands "in mute despair" as help was summoned. Doctors Robert Gibbes and A. N. Talley came. The crisis passed. They forbade Timrod to speak, as a recurrence of bleeding had to be prevented at all costs. The patient wrote a note to Emily. "I had just thought out a verse of what would have been a fine poem, when I was seized." The sensation he felt when bleeding was like "that of being in the grip of a monster from which there was no escape."[19]

Three days later Emily could report encouraging news to Hayne. There had been no further loss of blood and Timrod was stronger than his physicians expected. A letter and gift of a coin from little Willie Hayne was much appreciated. Katie was proving to be a good nurse, "although anxiety and excitement have faded the roses of her cheek." What Emily did not mention in this letter was that Katie was expecting another child.[20]

In a week Timrod was able to get out of bed for a few hours each day. Still, the fear never left him and his family that bleeding would return. At two o'clock on the morning of Wednesday, October 2 he touched Katie, sleeping by his side. "It is come," he said. Emily awakened to witness once more "the life stream flowing from his lips." Though the bleeding finally stopped, symptoms of pneumonia soon made their appearance. The two doctors did all that medical science had taught them. Their patient was "cupped and blistered" and periodically administered morphine. By Friday morning Dr. Gibbes realized that hope was gone. "Mr. Timrod," he said to the sufferer, "I think it my duty to tell you that I can see no chance of your recovery."

"Never shall I forget the fearfully startled expression of my brother's face at this announcement," said Emily. The doctor departed. Timrod turned to his sister. "And is this to be the end of all? So soon, and I have achieved so little? . . . And then I have loved you all so much. Oh! how *can* I leave you?" He wondered if he might *will* himself to live. That night Hugh Thompson stayed at his bedside, talking to Emily, and keeping him company. "I have enjoyed this night," Timrod said in the morning, "I slept when I wanted and listened when I liked." A New Testament was kept by his pillow. He often asked Emily to read to him from the Gospels and to pray.

Saturday morning he rested comfortably. William Rivers, Timrod's teacher from long ago, came to visit and found him seemingly unchanged, "still almost a child in simplicity of demeanor and purity of sentiment." Pain returned in the afternoon. At two o'clock Sunday morning Timrod awoke in great distress and convulsions began to wrack his body. "To listen to those groans, those shrieks was unutterable horror; was agony untold," said Emily. "For hours the struggle lasted, and then came for a short space rest, and consciousness . . . In the early hours of that Sabbath morning, the holy communion was administered to him by a clergyman of our Church." Timrod whispered remembrances for those absent: to Paul Hayne and his family; to nieces Katie, Edith, and Anna; to John Bruns and George Bryan. He urged all to "give attention to religion in life." Several times Timrod repeated the words of Charles Wesley's hymn, "Jesus, Lover of My Soul."

"Is it Sunday?" Timrod asked Emily. "I shall spend then my Sabbath in Eternity." He quoted a line from a short poem he had written a decade earlier entitled "A Common Thought," and asked if Emily remembered. It dealt with contemplation of death's "solemn day." "Yes and now that hour is come," she tearfully replied.

He folded his arms as if a spectator. "So this is Death. How strange to watch the struggle! It appears like two tides, two tides advancing and receding. These powers of Life and Death."

Everyone in the room was weeping except Timrod. Soon convulsions came again and it took two men to hold him down. He then slept until midnight, again with the help of morphine. Awakening, he asked one at his bedside to move a little so as not to block his view. He was certain that he saw Rebecca, Willie, and George Goodwin in the room.

"He seemed consumed by an unquenchable thirst," said Emily. "Nothing allayed that dreadful torture." She gave him water and tried to comfort him. He reminded her of lines from Shakespeare's *King John* that he had read to her some weeks earlier, impressed then by the "force of the words."

> I am a scribbled form, drawn with a pen
> Upon a parchment; and against this fire
> Do I shrink up.
>
> . . . .
>
> And none of you will bid the winter come,
> To thrust his icy fingers in my maw;

"Darling," said Emily, "you will soon be at rest."

"Yes, but love is sweeter than rest," he replied.

It was nearly dawn, Monday, October 7, 1867 when Katie attempted to give her husband one more spoonful of water. He was unable to take it. "Never mind," whispered Timrod. "I shall soon drink of the river of eternal life."[21]

"My dear dear friend," Emily wrote Hayne the next day, "our brother is with God."[22]

12

"He had the true fire within"

"IT IS WITH UNFEIGNED REGRET AND SORROW," JULIAN A. SELBY wrote in his *Daily Phoenix,* "that we make the announcement of the death of our young and gifted friend, Henry Timrod, Esq." The funeral was held at Trinity Church at four o'clock on the afternoon of Tuesday, October 8. Rev. Peter Shand was ill, but present. The service was conducted by Rev. C. Bruce Walker, the man who had served communion to Timrod two days earlier. "We brought nothing into this world, and it is certain we can carry nothing out," read Walker from The Order for the Burial of the Dead. "The LORD gave, and the LORD hath taken away; blessed be the name of the LORD." Pallbearers were: General Wade Hampton; A. N. Talley, M. D.; Robert W. Gibbes, M. D.; Hugh Thompson; William H. Talley; Felix G. De Fontaine; Melvin Cohen; and James S. Simons. Timrod was laid to rest in Trinity's churchyard, beside the graves of Willie and Edith.

"Ma seems to feel it more than any other loss she has had," wrote Emily. "I must not omit to say that all that friendship could do was done. He wanted for nothing; delicacies poured in on him, but alas too late to do him any good. Mrs. Gibbes and Mrs. Talley, and Mr. Cohen were all with us that dreadful Sunday. And all that Monday and Tuesday we were not permitted to get any thing ourselves, every meal being sent us ready prepared. Even liquor for those who sat up."[1]

South Carolina newspapers mourned his passing, three publishing original verse in honor of Timrod. Only six days after his death the *Metropolitan Record* of New York published a poetic appreciation by Sallie A. Brock. Simms wrote a eulogy for *Southern Society.* While praising Timrod's genius, Simms was also critical. "His hope was small," said Simms. "He had none of the sanguine in his system."

"Never was [there] a more unjust estimate of character," Emily fumed. "Hal hopeless! Hal not sanguine! Why his trust in some good yet in store for him and for us was boundless." Professor Rivers delivered a lecture in the chapel of South Carolina College paying tribute to Timrod, recognition that brought a note of thanks signed by Emily and Katie. "Very dear to the heart of the gentle poet was the thought of posthumous fame . . ."[2]

Katie Timrod was in the early stages of pregnancy, but soon became ill. "Poor almost destitute as we are," Emily wrote to Paul Hayne's wife Mary, "I cannot but pray that our hopes may not be disappointed; that an inheritor to the name and genius of our Southern poet may yet be given us." It was not to be. Before the end of October Katie had lost the child.[3]

Almost immediately after Timrod's death friends proposed to collect and publish his poetry, including in that volume a biographical sketch. Most thought that Judge Bryan should complete and edit the work, but Emily Goodwin would have none of it. Hayne claimed that right and Emily agreed, adamant that the book "can be confided to no better hands than those of his truest friend."[4] Emily sent the proof sheets to Hayne, but asked to have them returned after the book was published. "It is the only copy we have, and was given to Katie before her marriage and prized highly by her. It was by my darling's bedside the morning of that fearful hemorrhage, and has some of the crimson life drops on its pages." She sent much biographical information to Hayne and he prepared a memoir of Timrod to be included as an introduction to the book. "In publishing the volume," wrote Emily, "let the poem to Katie be the first one in the collection."[5]

In a short time the work was complete, but Hayne could find no publishers willing to risk their own capital on the venture. It was the beginning of Radical Reconstruction, and not since the war itself had feelings against the "disloyal" South run so high. "The objection is," Hayne told Clara Dargan, "that the majority of his pieces, and the ablest, deal with Confederate topics, and praise Confederate heroes, and that the book would fall 'still born' upon the Northern Market." Hayne was able to publish his own nonpolitical verse while readily admitting that Timrod's work was superior. "Yet—Heaven is my witness when I declare that I would—rather, a hundred times over, have brought out Timrod's book than mine."[6]

Timrod, as no other poet, truly expressed the soul of the Confederate South. Yet he deserved to be remembered for more than his war-related poems, as brilliant as many of them are. Hayne well understood that Timrod's imagination, intensity, and genius of expression marked him as the foremost Southern poet of his generation.

Emily Goodwin moved to a rented house at the corner of Senate and Pickens streets and took in several U. S. Army officers as boarders. Little did she realize the repercussions. Her friends, "with the exception of a very few have utterly forsaken me," assuming "that I could not touch pitch, and remain undefiled, that association with 'Yankees' must necessarily make a Yankee of me. I am consequently isolated in Columbia." To his credit Simms, before his death in 1870, was one of those who continued to offer financial help to Emily Goodwin. And he lent his influence in an effort to find employment for Katie Timrod.[7] On April 15, 1870 Thyrza Timrod died. She had been in failing health for years, disappointed too that her son's work remained uncollected. "With regard to Hal's poems," Emily wrote to Hayne a few weeks after her mother's death, "I have long despaired of seeing them published."[8]

Katie applied for work with the U. S. Treasury Department in Washington, D. C., a year after her husband's death. She was put on a waiting list, but eventually secured the job—apparently clerical—at an annual salary of $960. Emily joined her in Washington, but soon learned that she was dying of cancer. "*Are* you suffering from the most terrible disease in the world," wrote Hayne, "with a certainty that your days draw rapidly to their close?" He gave Emily what spiritual encouragement he could.[9] And he reported that he had finally found a publisher for her brother's volume of poetry. E. J. Hale of New York, a North Carolinian by birth, took on the task. Emily was thrilled with the news, thanking Hayne for his "labor of love" and rejoicing to see galley proofs of the forthcoming book. Katie pronounced Hayne's memoir "just perfect," but feared for her job if it became known that she was the widow of the poet. "Hal's book is very rebel, and they will certainly hold it against me if they find out," she told him, terrified of being "set adrift in this hard north."[10]

Katie received her copy of the book on January 22, 1873, and immediately wrote to Hayne. "At last the work is done, and that which the poet so ardently wished is consummated. But Oh my friend! as I held the book in my hand, thick, blinding tears rushed to my eyes, and for the time all other feelings were merged in one of bitter, bitter pain. They, the loved and lost, who would have welcomed so gladly the precious volume, were not with me." Emily Goodwin had died October 14. "My sister, my noble sister, whose loss has made such a terrible blank in my life, cannot share with me in this achievement of our hopes. I alone of all the little band, that clung to each other so truly and fondly, am left. . . . To you who have so nobly fulfilled the task, which you undertook in such earnest love of your brother poet, what can I say. I find it *impossible* to tell you *all* the gratitude I feel to you, for your unremitting efforts to *secure* the fame of your dead friend."[11]

The South may have had a reputation, expressed by Edwin P. Whipple, for being "contemptuous of all talent which is not political." But the publication of Hayne's edition of Timrod's work met with astonishing success. Reviews were favorable. Sales were so good that the publisher brought out a second edition—one that included several additional poems—in April 1873. Hayne was more than gratified. "After years on years of disappointment, and 'hope' bitterly 'deferred,' I conquered the *malignant* fates, and brought my friend's genius to the knowledge of the literary public."[12]

Even before the publication of the volume, Hayne received encouraging correspondence from the Quaker poet John Greenleaf Whittier. "I want to tell thee how much I have admired the poems of thy f^d. Timrod. Some of his later poems—notwithstanding their hostility to my own section—were very powerful & impressive . . . He had the true fire within." Emily Goodwin remembered that her brother especially enjoyed Whittier's "Snow Bound," copying the verses at Hayne's home so he could read them to her.[13] Hayne assured Whittier that even in Timrod's war poetry "there is no real malignity. A kinder-hearted being never existed." During the middle of the war Whittier had shocked his friends—Ralph Waldo Emerson, Edwin P. Whipple, and Oliver Wendell Holmes—"by my enthusiastic praise of one or two of [Timrod's] poems which I had seen." Whittier hoped "that the time has fully come, when no sectional feeling, will interfere with the recognition of his genius." Holmes was sure that Timrod's merits were now "pretty generally recognized."[14]

Hayne was quick to defend Timrod against what he thought were slights or slanders. When editor Rossiter Johnson wrote in 1875 that Timrod "advocated secession," Hayne replied in a long letter claiming that his friend in fact "opposed secession."[15] With the passage of years many, like Hayne, tended to forget the political situation that existed in 1860 and before. Most had indeed opposed those original advocates of disunion—men such as Hayne himself—in the decades leading up to the election of Lincoln. But after that revolutionary event nearly all South Carolinians chose to abandon the Union, despite their prior caution. In 1877 Hayne responded to what he saw as Sidney Lanier's unjust criticism, in his book *Florida,* of Timrod's "technique of verse." "Excepting *Edgar Poe,*" wrote Hayne to Lanier, "I don't believe the Southern, nay, the American has ever existed, whose knowledge of the *'technique of verse'* surpassed Timrod's."[16]

Hayne corresponded too with Henry Wadsworth Longfellow, sending the poet a copy of Timrod's volume soon after it was published. Years later, in 1880, William A. Courtenay visited Boston. Courtenay was by then mayor of Charleston and was invited to a formal breakfast at the home of Robert C. Winthrop. Longfellow was another guest, and the two were introduced. "Before I could say half a dozen words," remembered Courtenay, "Mr. Longfellow took my hand in both of his, and with an expression of . . . earnestness and warmth I shall not forget, said: 'From Charleston, South Carolina! It is a distinct honor, sir, to meet the Mayor of that city that gave birth to Henry Timrod, for the day will surely come when the poems of your townsman will have a place in every cultivated home in the United States.'"[17]

Courtenay never forgot his promise made to Timrod at the Branchville railroad station in the waning days of the war. He claimed later that he found a publisher a year before Hayne did, and wanted Judge Bryan to write a memoir of Timrod for the volume. "How Mr. Hayne came into it, I never understood." In the intervening years demand for Timrod's work remained strong, though the Hayne edition was out of print, E. J. Hale having gone out of business. Paul Hayne died in 1886. There was talk in 1894 and 1896 of producing a new edition.[18] Finally, Mayor Courtenay would found the Timrod Memorial Association. Chartered by the state of South Carolina, it was supported by a large group of university scholars and other leaders. The Association's goal was to publish a new edition of the poet's work. With money earned they hoped to remember Timrod with the erection of monuments.

Arrangements were made with Houghton, Mifflin & Company to publish a handsome volume, illustrated with a frontispiece portrait of Timrod. At a cost of $1.50 each, subscribers were encouraged to place advance orders. The book came out in April 1899 and soon all 4,000 copies were sold. Royalties were sufficient for the Association to erect a new cemetery marker on the poet's grave in Columbia. And with impressive ceremonies the Charleston monument was dedicated in the first year of the twentieth century.[19]

During the publicity surrounding the publication of the "memorial edition" Courtenay received many letters. One was from a woman in Springhill, near Mobile, Alabama. "I was hardly out of my teens when I first met Timrod, and of course, could not appreciate his rare gifts . . . But even then, I wondered at his unaffected unselfish interest, his unassuming amusement." She was pained "to recall how I aired my theories, and recklessly even criticized and found fault with him and his work." She still treasured the letters that Timrod had written her and considered herself one of "his loving friends." Her name was Rachel Lyons Heustis.[20]

Katie Timrod would in middle age marry English immigrant Alfred Lloyd. She too was pleased with the "memorial edition." Courtenay's last act as president of the Association was to sell the book's copyright, plates, and 200 unbound copies to the B. F. Johnson Company of Richmond for $1,000. This sum he presented to Katie Timrod Lloyd. She died on February 20, 1913, at Ridgefield Park, New Jersey.[21]

❧ ❧ ❧

The sun set and the crowd dispersed after the May 1901 ceremony of dedication in Charleston's Washington Park. Just above the floral tribute at the base of Timrod's monument, on the west side, was a bronze panel bearing an inscription.

Through clouds and through sunshine, in peace and in war, amid the stress of poverty and the storms of civil strife, his soul never faltered and his purpose never failed. To his poetic mission he was faithful to the end. In life and in death he was "not disobedient unto the Heavenly vision."[22]

Notes

ABBREVIATIONS USED IN THE NOTES

Because a number of sources appear frequently, the following abbreviations have been adopted. Other sources are cited fully in the notes.

Collected   Timrod, Henry. *The Collected Poems of Henry Timrod: A Variorum Edition*. Edited by Edd Winfield Parks and Aileen Wells Parks. Athens: University of Georgia Press, 1965.

CSR-SC   Compiled Service Records of Confederate Soldiers Who Served in Organizations from the State of South Carolina. U. S. National Archives, Washington, D. C.

Fidler   Fidler, William, ed. "Unpublished Letters of Henry Timrod." *The Southern Literary Messenger,* 2 (October, November, December, 1940).

Hayne   Hayne, Paul H. "Memoir of Henry Timrod." In Timrod, Henry. *The Poems of Henry Timrod.* Edited by Paul H. Hayne. New York: E. J. Hale & Son, Publishers, 1873.

HTP-SCL   Timrod, Henry. Papers. South Caroliniana Library, University of South Carolina, Columbia, S. C.

Hubbell   Hubbell, Jay B., ed. *The Last Years of Henry Timrod 1864–1867.* Durham: Duke University Press, 1941.

Oliphant   Oliphant, Mary C. Simms, Alfred Taylor Odell, and T. C. Duncan Eaves, eds. *The Letters of William Gilmore Simms.* 6 vols. Columbia: University of South Carolina Press, 1955–1982.

SSP-SCL   Sosnowski-Schaller Family. Papers. South Caroliniana Library, University of South Carolina, Columbia, S. C.

Uncollected   Timrod, Henry. *The Uncollected Poems of Henry Timrod,* edited by Guy A. Cardwell, Jr. Athens: University of Georgia Press, 1942.

Wauchope   Wauchope, George Armstrong. "Henry Timrod: Man and Poet, A Critical Study." *Bulletin of the University of South Carolina* 41, part 4 (April 1915).

The following abbreviations are used in the correspondence:

ETG   Emily Timrod Goodwin

HT   Henry Timrod

KT   Katie Timrod

PHH   Paul Hamilton Hayne

RL   Rachel Lyons

WGS   William Gilmore Simms

CHAPTER 1. "THAT BOY WILL, IF HE LIVES, BE A POET"

1. *News and Courier,* 2 May 1901; "Notes and Queries—Timrod," *South Carolina Historical and Genealogical Magazine* 2, (1901), 250; undated [May 1901] clipping from *Nashville Banner* (William H. Wills Papers, Southern Historical Collection, University of North Carolina).

2. A. S. Salley, Jr., *The History of Orangeburg County South Carolina* (Baltimore: Regional Publishing Company, 1978), 29–30; Timrod Memorial Association, *Proceedings at the Unveiling of the Art Memorial in Washington Square, Charleston, South Carolina, May-Day, 1901* (Charleston: Lucas & Richardson Co., n.d.), 28. The modern spelling of South Carolina localities is given throughout this book.

3. George J. Congaware, *The History of the German Friendly Society of Charleston, South Carolina, 1766–1916* (Richmond: Garrett & Massie, Publishers, 1935), 7, 10–11, 15–16; The History of the Synod Committee, *A History of the Lutheran Church in South Carolina* (Columbia: The R. L. Bryan Company, 1971), 76; Memorial Association, *Proceedings,* 28.

4. George C. Rogers, Jr., *Charleston in the Age of the Pinckneys* (Norman: University of Oklahoma Press, 1969), 4, 7–9, 17–18, 27–29, 141.

5. Congaware, *Friendly Society,* 1; Memorial Association, *Proceedings,* 30.

6. Rogers, *Charleston,* 86–87, 141; Memorial Association, *Proceedings,* 30; "Poll Lists Charleston Municipal Elections 1787," *South Carolina Historical Magazine* 56, (1955), 46.

7. Memorial Association, *Proceedings,* 31; Mabel L. Webber, compiler, "Marriage and Death Notices From the South Carolina Weekly Gazette," *The South Carolina Historical and Genealogical Magazine* 19, (1918), 108; A. S. Salley, Jr., ed. and compiler, *Marriage Notices in the South-Carolina Gazette and its Successors 1732–1801* (Baltimore: Genealogical Publishing Co., 1965), 75–76; Estate Record of Henry Timrod, 22 June 1783 (General Index, Miscellaneous Records of Bills of Sale, 1729–1825, South Carolina Department of Archives and History).

8. ETG to PHH, 2 December 1867 (HTP-SCL); Memorial Association, *Proceedings,* 31. Hayne gives Susannah's maiden name as "Graham," misinformation he received from Katie Timrod. KT to PHH, 5 June 1872 (PHH Papers, Duke University).

9. Caroline T. Moore, ed. and compiler, *Abstracts of Wills of Charleston District South Carolina 1783–1800* (Columbia: R. L. Bryan Co., 1974), 317; Hayne, 8; James W. Hagy, ed., *City Directories for Charleston, South Carolina for the Years 1803, 1806, 1807, 1809, and 1813* (Baltimore: Clearfield Co., 1995), 134; ETG to PHH, 2 December 1867 (HTP-SCL).

10. Congaware, *Friendly Society,* 43; ETG to PHH, 2 December 1867 (HTP-SCL).

11. Hayne, 9.

12. Memorial Association, *Proceedings,* 31; Congaware, *Friendly Society,* 73; paper of J. A. Leo Lemay (William Henry Timrod Papers, South Carolina Historical Society).

13. Hubbell, 172–176.

14. ETG to PHH, 15 September 1867 (HTP–SCL).

15. Memorial Association, *Proceedings,* 25–26; Hayne, 41n. For the story—and its refutation—that Faesch's grandmother was "a free person of color" see Rupert Taylor, "Henry Timrod's Ancestress, Hannah Caesar," *American Literature* 9, (January 1938): 419–430.

16. Virginia Pettigrew Clare, *Harp of the South* (Atlanta: Oglethorpe University Press, 1936), 25. Clare received her information in correspondence with family members. ETG to PHH, 25 September 1872 (HTP-SCL); unidentified, undated newspaper clipping in scrapbook (HTP-SCL).

17. G. A. Cardwell, Jr., "The Date of Henry Timrod's Birth," *American Literature* 7 (May 1935): 207–208. Cardwell discovered Henry Timrod's birth (8 December 1828) carefully recorded in his father's daybook in the Charleston Library Society. That document was lost before 1964.

18. Hayne, 12–14.

19. ETG to PHH, 25 September 1872 (HTP-SCL); Clare, *Harp,* 26–27. A Goodwin descendant related the anecdote to Clare in a 1935 letter.

CHAPTER 2. "BLUE SKIES ABOVE ME, BUT A MIST AHEAD"

1. Walter Brian Cisco, *Taking a Stand: Portraits From the Southern Secession Movement* (Shippensburg, Pa.: White Mane Books, 1998), 7, 27, 32–37.

2. Hubbell, 173–174; Hayne, 15–16.

3. Clipping from unidentified newspaper, 22 August 1834, in scrapbook (HTP-SCL); Cisco, *Stand,* 36.

4. William W. Freehling, *Prelude to Civil War: The Nullification Controversy in South Carolina 1816–1836* (New York: Oxford University Press, 1966), 309–10; unidentified newspaper clipping, n. d., scrapbook (HTP-SCL).

5. George T. Congaware, *The History of the German Friendly Society of Charleston, South Carolina, 1766–1916* (Richmond: Garrett & Massie, Publishers, 1935), 196; Guy A. Cardwell, Jr., "William Henry Timrod, The Charleston Volunteers, and the Defense of St. Augustine," *The North Carolina Historical Review* 18, no. 1 (January 1941): 27.

6. Hubbell, 175; W[illiam] H[enry] T[imrod], "Scenes From an Unpublished Drama," *Southern Literary Journal* 1, no. 4 (December 1835): 270–273; W[illiam]

H[enry] T[imrod], "Scenes From an Unpublished Drama," *The Southern Rose* 5, no. 25 (5 August 1837): 200.

7. Hubbell, 155, 176–77 (McCarter's punctuation has been regularized); John Caldwell Guilds, *Simms: A Literary Life* (Fayetteville: University of Arkansas Press, 1992), 34.

8. John K. Mahon, *History of the Second Seminole War, 1835–1842* (Gainesville: University of Florida Press, 1985), 135–136; Statement of William Henry Timrod, 26 September 1836 (William A. Courtenay Collection, Charleston Library Society); John T. Sprague, *The Origin, Progress, and Conclusion of the Florida War* (New York: D. Appleton & Company, 1848), 10.

9. Cardwell, Jr., "Charleston Volunteers," 37; Hubbell, 176.

10. Bernhard, Duke of Saxe–Weimar–Eisenach, *Travels by His Highness Duke Bernhard of Saxe–Weimar–Eisenach through North America in the Years 1825 and 1826* (Lanham, Md.: University Press of America, 2001), 288–89.

11. Hayne, 17–18; Colyer Meriwether, *History of Higher Education in South Carolina With a Sketch of the Free School System* (Washington: Government Printing Office, 1889), 30–32, 35. Hayne leaves the impression that he and Timrod began their education at the same school (Hayne, 17). Another remembered Hayne having attended one school before Cotes' (Meriwether, *Education,* 35).

12. Uncollected, 53–54, 117. "Not a Grin Was Seen," in Timrod's Autographic Relics in the Charleston Library Society, bears the date 1844 and "First known effort Written at 15." This is contradicted by the 1843 date found on "In Bowers of Ease." (See Uncollected, 115, 119.)

CHAPTER 3. "HARRY, YOU ARE A FOOL!

1. Hayne, 18; Daniel Walker Hollis, *University of South Carolina.* 2 vols. Volume 1: *South Carolina College* (Columbia: University of South Carolina Press, 1951), 149, 153, 172.

2. *Southern Banner,* 16 January 1845 and 10 April 1845; Lester Hargrett, "Student Life at the University of Georgia in the 1840s," *The Georgia Historical Quarterly* 8, no. 1 (March 1924): 55; Virginia Pettigrew Clare, *Harp of the South* (Atlanta: Oglethorpe University Press, 1936), 30; Edd Winfield Parks, "Timrod's College Days," *American Literature* 7 (November 1936): 294–295. Clare's authority for her reference to Ross came in a 1936 letter from Alexander S. Salley of the Historical Commission of S. C.

3. *Southern Banner,* 10 April 1845; Hargrett, "Student Life," 49, 50, 52; Thomas G. Dyer, *The University of Georgia: A Bicentennial History, 1785–1985* (Athens: University of Georgia Press, 1985), 10, 36–37, 47, 50, 79–80.

4. Hargrett, "Student Life," 55–56; Dyer, *Georgia,* 60, 61, 63–64; *Southern Banner,* 3 July 1845 and 11 August 1846; Parks, "College Days," 295.

5. Dyer, *Georgia,* 53; Parks, "College Days," 295; Hayne, 18, 19.

6. Uncollected, 79, 119.

7. Ibid., 40, 116.

8. Ibid., 55, 118; Hargrett, "Student Life," 52.

9. Uncollected, 59, 118.

10. Ibid., 115; E. Merton Coulter, *College Life in the Old South* (Athens: University of Georgia Press, 1983), 130; Clare, *Harp*, 30. In a 1935 letter to Clare, Alexander S. Salley of the Historical Commission of S. C. related what he had learned years earlier from an Athens professor about Timrod's reputation.

11. Hargrett, "Student Life," 53; Dyer, *Georgia*, 46; Clare, *Harp*, 35.

12. Ibid. The description is from a letter from Joseph H. Mellichamp to Robert E. Mellichamp, 18 April 1899. Clare includes only part within quotation marks although it seems clear that the entire statement was Mellichamp's.

13. Hayne, 19; Parks, "College Days," 294–96; Clare, *Harp*, 34n. Clare quotes a 1935 letter to her from the University registrar: "I find nothing to indicate that Henry Timrod was ever dismissed from the University of Georgia for misconduct."

14. Hayne, 19.

15. Census of 1850, Charleston District, S. C. (U.S. National Archives). The census– taker was given Timrod's correct age on 12 September 1850, additional evidence that he was indeed born in 1828. Hayne, 19–20; *News and Courier*, 30 April 1899; Clare, *Harp*, 36. Clare quotes a letter from Ursula S. Bird to William A. Courtenay, 10 June 1896.

16. Paul H. Hayne, "Ante-Bellum Charleston," *Southern Bivouac* 1, no. 6 (November 1885): 327–29; PHH to Margaret J. Preston, 10 May 1873, in Rayburn S. Moore, ed., *A Man of Letters in the Nineteenth Century South: Selected Letters of Paul Hamilton Hayne* (Baton Rouge: Louisiana State University Press, 1982), 113; Ward W. Briggs, Jr., ed., *The Letters of Basil Lanneau Gildersleeve* (Baltimore: The Johns Hopkins University Press, 1987), 5; Basil L. Gildersleeve, "Formative Influences," *The Forum* (February 1891): 607.

17. *News and Courier*, 20 December 1903.

18. Hayne, 19–20.

19. Collected, 142.

20. Ibid., 20.

21. Hayne, 21–22, 21n–22n.

Chapter 4. "Praecepter Amat"

1. Wauchope, 12, 14; KT to PHH, 5 June 1872 (PHH Papers, Duke University). Dr. Wauchope obtained his information from individuals who knew Timrod. The professor deleted the expletives in his narrative. Biographer Thompson is confused in his chronology of Timrod employers, and Clare follows Thompson.

2. Census of 1850, Colleton District, S. C. (U. S. National Archives); F. A. Sondley, *A History of Buncombe County, North Carolina* (Spartanburg, S. C.: The Reprint Company, 1977), 617; HT to ETG, 4 July 1851 (HTP-SCL).

3. Peggy B. Altman, et al., compilers, *1850 Census of Darlington County, South Carolina* (n. p.: privately printed, n. d.), 145; Census of 1860, Richland District, S. C. (U. S. National Archives). The census-taker misspelled their name as "Goodwyn," the name of a family prominent in Columbia.

4. HT to ETG, 3 October 1851 (HTP-SCL).

5. HT to ETG, 29 July 1853 (HTP-SCL).

6. HT to ETG, 3 October 1851 (HTP-SCL).

7. Uncollected, 109, 121.

8. Collected, 28, 148.

9. Ibid., 30, 151.

10. Hayne, 22–23; Rayburn S. Moore, *Paul Hamilton Hayne* (New York: Twayne Publishers, Inc., 1972), 17–19; PHH to Mary M. Michel, 7 September 1851 (PHH Papers, Duke University).

11. *News and Courier,* 20 December 1903; Hayne, 23; Wauchope, 13–15.

12. Collected, 31–32, 152.

13. Ibid., 29–30, 150.

14. Louis P. Towles, ed., *A World Turned Upside Down: The Palmers of South Santee, 1818–1881* (Columbia: University of South Carolina Press, 1996), 20, 1017.

15. D. M. McKeithan, "Paul Hamilton Hayne Writes to the Granddaughter of Patrick Henry," *Georgia Historical Quarterly* 32, no. 1 (March 1948): 24.

16. HT to Oscar T. Keeler, 10 April 1856, in Thomas Ollive Mabbott, ed., "Some Letters of Henry Timrod," *The American Collector* 3 (February 1927): 192; Census of 1850 and of 1860, Orangeburgh District, S. C. (U. S. National Archives); Daniel Marchant Culler, *Orangeburgh District, 1767–1868: History and Records* (Spartanburg, S. C.: The Reprint Company, 1995), 111, 147.

17. Ibid., 426, 427; Census of 1850, Schedule 2, Orangeburgh District, S. C. (U. S. National Archives).

18. *The Southron,* 30 April 1856.

19. HT to Oscar T. Keeler, 10 April 1856 in Mabbott, ed., "Letters," 192; Uncollected, 119; Wauchope, 13.

20. HT to Sarah [A. Prince], 12 October 1857 (HTP-SCL); Hayne, 23; Edgar Long, "Russell's Magazine As An Expression of Ante-Bellum South Carolina Culture" (PhD dissertation, University of South Carolina, 1932), 54.

21. Collected, 156; Richard Vaughn, *The Arctic: A History* (Gloucestershire: Allan Sutton Publishing Limited, 1994), 154–155, 170–174; George W. Corner, *Doctor Kane of the Arctic Seas* (Philadelphia: Temple University Press, 1972), 268–69; Elisha Kent Kane, *Arctic Explorations: The Second Grinnell Expedition in Search of Sir John Franklin* (Philadelphia: Childs & Peterson, 1856), 2: 57.

22. Collected, 36–37.

23. Ibid., 159.

24. HT to Sarah [A. Prince], 12 October 1857 (HTP-SCL).

25. Collected, 45, 46, 160.

26. HT to Sarah [A. Prince], 12 October 1857 (HTP-SCL); Collected, 53–56, 166.

27. HT to ETG, 12 March 1861 (HTP-SCL); Culler, *Orangeburgh,* 148; Wauchope, 12–13. Felicia Hurtel Robinson was born on 2 June 1847. She married Edward North Chisolm on 3 December 1874. See William Garnett Chisolm, *Chisolm Genealogy* (New York: The Knickerbocker Press, 1914), 33.

28. Henry T. Thompson, *Henry Timrod: Laureate of the Confederacy* (Columbia: The State Company, 1928), 21–22; Virginia Pettigrew Clare, *Harp of the South* (Atlanta: Oglethorpe University Press, 1936), 49–50; Census of 1850, Darlington District, S. C. (U.S. National Archives). Clare quotes a Goodwin descendant. Thompson's source was Sallie Cannon, a relative not found in the 1850 census.

29. Thompson, *Laureate*, 22–23; Clare, *Harp*, 50; Hayne, 43; Thomas Dormandy, *The White Death: A History of Tuberculosis* (New York: New York University Press, 2000), 1–61, passim. Hayne thought Kate arrived in 1860. Both Thompson and Clare received their information from grandchildren of Dr. Porcher. The final quote is from Sallie Cannon.

CHAPTER 5. "OUR YOUNG CAROLINA PETRARCH"

1. Henry Timrod, *The Essays of Henry Timrod*. Edited by Edd Winfield Parks. (Athens: University of Georgia Press, 1942), 61–62, 64, 65, 66, 157.

2. Ibid., 150, 151, 172.

3. Ibid., 69–70, 72, 75, 158.

4. Ibid., 84, 85, 89, 96, 97, 101–102, 160.

5. Edd Winfield Parks, *Henry Timrod* (New York: Twayne Publishers, 1964), 124n.

6. Henry Timrod, *Poems* (Boston: Ticknor and Fields, 1859); PHH to Richard Henry Stoddard, 14 February 1860 in Daniel Morley McKeithan, ed., *A Collection of Hayne Letters* (Austin: University of Texas Press, 1944), 5, 41; "Literary Notices," *Harper's New Monthly Magazine* 20, no. 118 (February 1860): 404; William P. Trent, *William Gilmore Simms* (Boston: Houghton Mifflin and Company, 1892), 233; Hubbell, 158.

7. Collected, 69–70, 73, 170.

8. Hayne, 42–43; Census of 1860, Richland District, S. C. (U. S. National Archives); HT to ETG, 10 February 1862 (HTP-SCL).

9. Daniel Walker Hollis, *University of South Carolina*. 2 vols. Volume 1: *South Carolina College* (Columbia: University of South Carolina Press, 1951), 207, 208; John Donald Wade, *Augustus Baldwin Longstreet: A Study of the Development of Culture in the South* (New York: MacMillan Company, 1924), 336; Edwin L. Green, *A History of the University of South Carolina* (Columbia: The State Company, 1916), 358.

10. Augustus Baldwin Longstreet to Sophia Wentz Sosnowski, 14 November 1860 SSP-SCL); clipping from *Athens Herald,* 10 December 1917; and unidentified, undated newspaper clipping (Sosnowski Family Scrapbook, South Caroliniana Library).

11. Sophie Sosnowski to Kallie Sosnowski, 19 January 1858 (SSP-SCL); Collected, 83–91, 177.

12. HT to Sophie Sosnowski, 29 April [1860] (HTP-SCL); Milledge B. Seigler, "Henry Timrod and Sophie Sosnowski," *The Georgia Historical Quarterly* 31, no. 3 (September 1947): 172-73.

13. Lawrence S. Rowland, et al., *The History of Beaufort County, South Carolina.* 2 vols. Volume 1: *1514–1861* (Columbia: University of South Carolina Press, 1996), 384; Wauchope, 14; HT to ETG, 8 May 1860 (HTP-SCL). The expletives are rendered as spoken, rather than as expurgated by Wauchope.

14. HT to ETG, 18 June 1860 (HTP-SCL); Collected, 177.

15. Walter Brian Cisco, *Taking a Stand: Portraits From the Southern Secession Movement* (Shippensburg, Pa.: White Mane Books, 1998), chapters 2 and 3; WGS to James Lawson, 10 November 1860 in Oliphant, 4: 260–61.

16. HT to ETG, 29 January 1861 (HTP–SCL).

CHAPTER 6. "HATH NOT THE MORNING
DAWNED WITH ADDED LIGHT?"

1. Census of 1860, Beaufort District, S. C. (U. S. National Archives); HT to ETG, 29 January 1861 (HTP-SCL).

2. William C. Davis, *"A Government of Our Own:" The Making of the Confederacy* (New York: The Free Press, 1994), 12, 71, 103, 109, 120.

3. Collected, 180; *The Living Age*, 30 March 1861; broadside (photocopy) "Ode," n. d. (HTP-SCL).

4. Collected, 92–95, 180; Hayne, 36–37.

5. HT to ETG, 12 March 1861 and 11 June 1861 (HTP-SCL); Frank Schaller to Sophie Sosnowski, 14 October 1860 and many other dates (SSP-SCL).

6. HT to ETG, 11 June 1861 (HTP-SCL); HT to RL, 29 May 1861 in Fidler, 532.

7. HT to RL, 9 June 1861 in Fidler, 533–535.

8. HT to RL, 7 July 1861 and 20 August 1861 in Fidler, 605, 607–608; Rachel Lyons Heustis to William A. Courtenay, 29 August 1900 (William A. Courtenay Papers, South Caroliniana Library).

9. Collected, 95–99, 183. "Ethnogenesis" and "The Cotton Boll" present the Confederacy as a redemptive community without making that community divine, according to one insightful scholar. Timrod's "Ode" (1866) borders on idolatry in its portrayal of "the ideological community of the lost cause." See James Randolph Loney, "The Poetry and Poetics of Henry Timrod, Paul Hamilton Hayne, and Sidney Lanier: An Essay on Art and Community in the Nineteenth–Century South," (PhD dissertation, University of Georgia, 1977), 60–61, 70, 71.

10. HT to RL, 6 September 1861 in Fidler, 608–609.

11. HT to RL, 10 December 1861 in William Fidler, ed., "Notes and Documents," *The Alabama Review* vol. II (April 1949): 140–141.

12. HT to RL, 25 December 1861 in Fidler, 609; Collected, 100, 105, 186.

13. HT to RL, 25 December 1861 in Fidler, 610; KT to PHH, 22 March 1878 (PHH Papers, Duke University).

14. HT to ETG, 4 January 1862 and 10 February 1862 (HTP-SCL).

15. HT to RL, 20 January 1862 in Fidler, 610-611.

16. HT to RL, 3 February 1862 in Fidler, 645; Collected, 106–107, 190.

17. HT to RL, 10 December 1861 in Fidler, ed., "Documents," 141; Henry Timrod Papers and Ainsley H. Cotchett Papers (CSR-SC); HT to RL, 3 February 1862 in Fidler, 646; Janet B. Hewett ed., *Supplement to the Official Records of the Union and Confederate Armies* (Wilmington, N. C.: Broadfoot Publishing Company, 1998), 65, part 1, 155, 159. Company B had originally been designated E.

18. HT to RL, 25 December 1861, 6 February 1862, and 21 February 1862 in Fidler, 610, 646, 647; HT to ETG, 21 February 1862 (HTP-SCL); Henry Timrod Papers (CSR-SC). An apparent misreading of Timrod's handwriting in his letter of February 6 has repeatedly identified him as being enrolled in the "30th Regiment," an organization that never existed.

19. HT to ETG, 21 February 1862 and 25 February 1862 (HTP-SCL).

20. HT to RL, 6 February 1862 in Fidler, 646–47; Collected, 109–111, 191, 192.

21. Hayne, 38.

CHAPTER 7. "ON DETACHED SERVICE"

1. Milby E. Burton, *The Siege of Charleston, 1861–1865* (Columbia: University of South Carolina Press, 1970), 84, 91–93, 124–26; unidentified newspaper clipping of letter dated 21 April 1862 in scrapbook (HTP-SCL).

2. HT to RL, 8 April 1862 in Fidler, 648–49; HT to ETG, 11 April 1862 (Thomas Ollive Mabbott Collection, Harry Ransom Humanities Research Center).

3. HT to RL, 21 February 1862 in Fidler, 648; HT to ETG, 11 April 1862 (Thomas Ollive Mabbott Collection, Harry Ransom Humanities Research Center); Henry Timrod Papers (CSR-SC).

4. HT to ETG, 11 April 1862 (Thomas Ollive Mabbott Collection, Harry Ransom Humanities Research Center); HT to RL, 15 April 1862 in Fidler, 650; HT to ETG, 15 April 1862 (HTP-SCL).

5. HT to RL, 15 April 1862 in Fidler, 650.

6. Unidentified newspaper clippings of dispatches dated 1, 2, 5, and 6 May [1862] in scrapbook (HTP-SCL); Shelby Foote, *The Civil War: A Narrative.* 3 vols. Volume 1: *Fort Sumter to Perryville* (New York: Vintage Books, 1986), 381–384.

7. T. C. De Leon, *Belles, Beaux, and Brains of the '60's* (New York: G.W. Dillingham Co., 1907), 184–85; unidentified newspaper clipping of statement made 19 April 1899 in Hubbell, 12–13; Hayne, 42.

8. Unidentified newspaper clippings, n. d., in scrapbook (HTP-SCL); Wauchope, 16.

9. C. Vann Woodward, ed., *Mary Chesnut's Civil War* (New Haven: Yale University Press, 1981), 389.

10. Ibid., 418-419.

11. HT to RL, 25 July 1862 in William Fidler, ed., "Notes and Documents," *The Alabama Review* 2 (April 1949): 143–44; Collected, 63; Uncollected, 120.

12. HT to John R. Thompson, 14 January 1863 (John R. Thompson Papers, Alderman Library); Oliphant, 1, cxxxix; Hayne, 38–39, 39n; HT to RL, 28 October 1862 in Fidler, ed., "Documents," 144–145.

13. Henry Timrod Papers (CSR–SC); Muster Roll/Pay Roll, Co. B, 20th S. C. Volunteers, 1 July 1862—31 August 1862 (South Caroliniana Library).

14. Collected, 194; Ellison Capers, *Confederate Military History Extended Edition.* Volume VI: *South Carolina* (Wilmington, NC: Broadfoot Publishing Company, 1987), 418.

15. Collected, 115–16, 194.

16. Ibid., 116–18, 195.

CHAPTER 8. "CHANCE FOR A WHILE
SHALL SEEM TO REIGN"

1. KT to PHH, 8 September 1872 in Hubbell, 35; Hayne, 39; HT to Edith Goodwin, 29 April [1863] (HTP-SCL).

2. Hayne, 38–39; Henry Vizetelly, *Glances Back Through Seventy Years: Autobiographical and Other Reminiscences.* 2 vols. (London: Kegan, Paul, Trench, Trubner, &

Co., Ltd., 1893), 2: 82, 85–86, 90–91, 95–96; Stanley W. Hoole, *Vizetelly Covers the Confederacy* (Tuscaloosa, Ala.: Confederate Publishing Company, Inc., 1957), 19, 20, 63.

3. HT to John R. Thompson, 14 January 1863 (John R. Thompson Papers, Alderman Library); HT to PHH, 11 July 1867 in Hubbell, 88; Collected, 121–22, 195–96.

4. Ibid., 122–23, 196.

5. Ibid., 125–26, 197.

6. Ibid., 127–29, 198.

7. HT to ETG, n.d. (HTP-SCL); HT to RL, 23 July 1863 in Fidler, 650.

8. Fitzgerald Ross, *A Visit to the Cities and Camps of the Confederate States* (London: W. Blackwood, 1865), 108, 120, 122.

9. Armistead Churchill Gordon, *Memories and Memorials of William Gordon McCabe* (Richmond: Old Dominion Press, 1925), 1: 132; Claude C. Sturgill and Charles L. Price, "McCabe's Impression of the Bombardment of Charleston, 1863," *South Carolina Historical Magazine* 71 (1970): 268–69.

10. Hoole, *Vizetelly*, 106–7; Ross, *Visit*, 179, 180.

11. Hayne, 40, 40n; unidentified, undated newspaper clipping in scrapbook (HTP-SCL); William Gordon McCabe to Richard H. Stoddard, 25 May 1873 (William Gordon McCabe Papers, Alderman Library). Not until August of the next year did Timrod finally acknowledge that "the project of publishing my poems in England has been silently but altogether dropped. It *is* a disappointment, of course, but I grin & bear it, as the lot of a poor poet." HT to PHH, 25 August [1864], in Hubbell, 43.

12. HT to RL, 23 July 1863 in Fidler, 651; HT to RL, 21 June 1863 and 12 August 1863 in William Fidler, ed., "Notes and Documents," *The Alabama Review* 2 (April 1949): 146.

13. HT to PHH, 20 July 1864 in Hubbell, 37; KT to PHH, 8 September 1873, in Hubbell, 35; Hubbell, 18n.

14. Henry Timrod, *The Essays of Henry Timrod*, edited by Edd Winfield Parks (Athens: University of Georgia Press, 1942), 112–13, 118–19, 165; Katie Timrod Lloyd to William A. Courtenay, 16 March 1901 (William A. Courtenay Collection, Charleston Library Society).

15. Kate Harbes Becker, *Paul Hamilton Hayne: Life and Letters* (Belmont, N. C.: The Outline Company, 1951), 38–39.

CHAPTER 9. "WE MAY NOT FALTER"

1. HT to PHH, 20 July 1864, in Hubbell, 37; Julian A. Selby, *Memorabilia and Anecdotal Reminiscences of Columbia, South Carolina* (Columbia: The R. L. Bryan Company, 1905), 101; Uncollected, 102–103, 120.

2. William Franciscus West, Jr., "A Southern Editor Views the Civil War: A Collection of Editorials By Henry Timrod and Other Editorial Materials Published in the *Daily South Carolinian*, January 14, 1864, to February 17, 1865" (PhD dissertation, Florida State University, 1984), pp 2, 17, 31. Though nothing in the newspaper is signed, West assumes—reasonably, based on the evidence—that Timrod wrote all or nearly all of the material compiled in this dissertation.

3. Ibid., 21, 22, 33, 34, 287.

4. Ibid., 42–43, 44, 181; Joseph H. Mellichamp to Robert E. Mellichamp, 18 April 1899, in Virginia Pettigrew Clare, *Harp of the South* (Atlanta: Oglethorpe University Press, 1936), pp 71–72.

5. Clippings from *Daily South Carolinian* [February 1864] (William A. Courtenay Collection, Charleston Library Society); clippings from *Portfolio*, 24 February 1864 (HTP-SCL); Albert Sidney Thomas, *A Historical Account of the Protestant Episcopal Church in South Carolina 1820–1957* (Columbia: R. L. Bryan Co., 1957), 518.

6. WGS to PHH, 8 May 1864, in Oliphant, 4: 450–451.

7. HT to PHH, 10 July 1864 and 20 July 1864 in Hubbell, 31–32, 37; HT to Clara Dargan, 20 August [1864], in Hubbell, 41.

8. West, "Southern Editor," 207, 299–300, 545–46, 547–48.

9. Ibid., 173, 174–75.

10. Ibid., 113.

11. Ibid., 447–48, 467, 468–469.

12. WGS to PHH, [ca. 1 August 1864] and 5 September [1864], in Oliphant, 4: 46 and 6, 234–35.

13. HT to PHH, 25 August [1864], in Hubbell, 41–42.

14. Unidentified newspaper clipping, [September 1864], in scrapbook (HTP-SCL); ETG to Frank Schaller, 30 July 1867 (SSP-SCL).

15. West, "Southern Editor," 815, 825, 836–37, 923–24, 925.

16. Collected, 198; West, "Southern Editor," 596–97, 598.

17. Hayne, 44, 45; unidentified, [October 1865], newspaper clipping in scrapbook (HTP–SCL).

CHAPTER 10. "O SADDEST CHILD OF TIME"

1. Statement of William A. Courtenay, 7 October 1902 (William A. Courtenay Papers, South Caroliniana Library); *Timrod Souvenir* (Aiken, S. C.: Palmetto Press, 1901), 13–14; William A. Courtenay Papers (CSR–SC); Yates Snowden, *History of South Carolina* 4 (Chicago: Lewis Publishing Co., 1920): 7.

2. Michael Fellman, *Citizen Sherman: A Life of William Tecumseh Sherman* (New York: Random House, 1995), 224–25; Julian A. Selby, *Memorabilia and Anecdotal Reminiscences of Columbia, South Carolina* (Columbia: R. L. Bryan Company, 1905), 101.

3. Hayne, 45; Albert Sidney Thomas, *A Historical Account of the Protestant Episcopal Church in South Carolina 1820–1957* (Columbia: R. L. Bryan Co., 1957), 518–19; Walter Brian Cisco, *Wade Hampton: Confederate Warrior, Conservative Statesman* (Dulles, Va.: Brassey's, Inc., 2004), chapter 11.

4. HT to Richard H. Stoddard, 10 July 1865 (Anthony Collection, Manuscripts and Archives Section, New York Public Library). Timrod probably did not literally take an oath. There is no evidence that he applied for a presidential pardon. See Case files for applications from former Confederates for Presidential pardons (U. S. National Archives).

5. Richard H. Stoddard to James T. Fields, 7 August 1865 (Richard H. Stoddard Papers, Alderman Library).

6. HT to [Richard H. Stoddard], 8 September 1865 (Anthony Collection, Manuscripts and Archives Section, New York Public Library).

7. Unidentified newspaper clippings, [October 1865 and May 1866], in scrapbook (HTP-SCL).

8. HT to PHH, 30 March 1866, in Hubbell, 59-61; William P. Trent, *William Gilmore Simms* (Boston: Houghton, Mifflin and Company, 1892), 292.

9. Unidentified newspaper clippings, [October 1865], in scrapbook (HTP-SCL); Hayne, 45n.

10. Collected, 133, 134-135.

11. "Anecdotes about our literary men," 1901 (William James Rivers Papers, South Caroliniana Library).

12. HT to PHH, 30 March 1866, in Hubbell, 59–61. This and other letters quoted by Hayne in his "Memoir" are highly embellished by that author.

13. *Daily South Carolinian,* 31 December 1865. Many have mistakenly assumed that Timrod referred to 1866 as "the old year."

14. Hayne, 47–51; KT to PHH, 10 September 1872 (PHH Papers, Duke University). Hayne reprinted two articles ("Spring's Lessons" and "Names of the Months Phonetically Expressive") that he correctly believed that Timrod wrote for the *Carolinian* post–war. One other, "The Alabama," which he thought was written during the war, was in fact published on 20 January 1866. Hayne was given these clippings by Katie and told they were Timrod's. Nothing in that paper is signed, but these are probably the only articles written by Timrod after the war for the *Carolinian.*

15. HT to PHH, 30 March 1866, in Hubbell, 62; KT to PHH, 9 February 1873 (PHH Papers, Duke University); *Daily Courier,* 13 February 1866.

16. HT to Edith Goodwin, 16 April [1866] (HTP-SCL).

17. WGS to William Hawkins Ferris, 24 March [1866], in Oliphant 4: 547; HT to PHH, 7 March 1866 in Hubbell, 55n, 55, 56.

18. ETG to PHH, 23 November 1867 (HTP-SCL); Snowden, *History* 2: 877; "Anecdotes about our literary men," 1901 (William James Rivers Papers, South Caroliniana Library).

19. Hayne, 54.

20. *Daily Courier,* 12, 14, and 18 June 1866; program, 16 June 1866 (Ladies' Association to Commemorate the Confederate Dead, South Caroliniana Library); C. P. Voigt, "New Light on Timrod's 'Memorial Ode,'" *American Literature* 4 (January 1933): 395–96; Collected, 129–30.

CHAPTER 11. "LOVE IS SWEETER THAN REST"

1. WGS to William Hawkins Ferris, 7 August 1866 and WGS to PHH, 22 October 1866 in Oliphant 4: 591–592.

2. Hubbell, 63–64, 67.

3. ETG to Sophie Schaller, 10 September 1866 (HTP-SCL); Sophie Schaller to ETG, 12 September 1866 and ETG to Sophie Schaller, 8 February 1867 (SSP-SCL).

4. *Daily Phoenix,* 23 September 1866.

5. HT to PHH, 19 November 1866, in Hubbell, 68; "Anecdotes about our literary men," 1901 (William James Rivers Papers, South Caroliniana Library);

Henry T. Thompson, *Henry Timrod: Laureate of the Confederacy* (Columbia: The State Company, 1928), 43; unidentified, undated newspaper clipping of Hugh S. Thompson letter, 27 January 1898 (William A. Courtenay Papers, South Caroliniana Library). Thompson (*Laureate*, 43) says that Timrod was defeated in an 1866 vote by state lawmakers for the position of messenger in the House. There is no record of a vote involving Timrod for "messenger" or for anything else. See *Journal of the House of Representatives of the State of South Carolina Being the Regular Session of 1866* (Columbia: F. G. De Fontaine, State Printer, 1866).

6. HT to PHH, 19 November 1866 in Hubbell, 69.

7. KT to PHH, 13 March 1873, in Hubbell, 64–66; unidentified, undated newspaper clipping of a letter in the Boston *Daily Advertiser*, 20 February 1873 (HTP-SCL); Wauchope, 17; WGS to PHH, 3 April 1867, in Hubbell, 78-79. In 1878 Hampton tried to find employment in Washington for Katie, even promising to go to the President. See KT to PHH, 22 March 1878 (PHH Papers, Duke University).

8. WGS to PHH, 3 April 1867, in Hubbell, 78–79; HT to PHH, 4 June [1867] in Hubbell, 83–84; ETG to PHH, 25 November 1867 (HTP-SCL).

9. ETG to Sophie Schaller, 4 February 1867 (HTP-SCL).

10. HT to PHH, 26 March [1867] (Henry Timrod Papers, Alderman Library). Thompson (*Laureate*, 48) says that Timrod underwent "a most painful and dangerous operation" in the spring of 1867. He gives no details and there is no corroborating evidence.

11. HT to John R. Thompson, 15 March 1867 and 15 April [1867] (Anthony Collection, Manuscripts and Archives Section, New York Public Library); John R. Thompson to PHH, 22 March 1867, in Hubbell, 73.

12. HT to PHH, 13 April 1867 (William A. Courtenay Papers, Charleston Library Society); Rayburn S. Moore, *Paul Hamilton Hayne* (New York: Twayne Publishers, 1972), 21–22; PHH to Edward Spencer, 20 March 1872 (Paul Hamilton Hayne Papers, Alderman Library).

13. Hayne, 54–55; Mary M. Hayne to ETG, January [1868] (HTP-SCL); HT to PHH, 11 July 1867, in Hubbell, 87-89.

14. HT to Frank Schaller, 3 August 1867 (HTP-SCL); KT to [Caroline Sosnowski], 4 August 1867 (SSP-SCL).

15. HT to PHH, 11 July 1867 and HT to Clara Dargan, 7 August 1867, in Hubbell, 88-89.

16. Hayne, 55–57; HT to ETG, 20 August [1867] and HT to ETG, undated fragment [August 1867] (HTP–SCL); HT to PHH, 13 September 1867 (Henry Timrod Letters, Princeton University).

17. Ibid.; Thompson, *Laureate*, 48–49; HT to PHH, 16 September [1867] (Henry Timrod Letters, Princeton University); unidentified, undated newspaper clipping of Hugh S. Thompson letter, 27 January 1898 (William A. Courtenay Papers, South Caroliniana Library).

18. Collected, 140, 202.

19. Hubbell, 92n; ETG to PHH, 20 September 1867 and 29 September 1867 (HTP–SCL).

20. ETG to PHH, 23 September 1867 and 15 October 1867 (HTP-SCL).

21. ETG to PHH, 22 October 1867 and ETG to [Edith Goodwin], 29 October 1867 (HTP-SCL); William J. Rivers, *A Little Book: To Obtain Means for Placing a*

Memorial Stone Upon the Grave of the Poet Henry Timrod (Charleston: Walker, Evans & Cogswell, n.d.), 8; *King John,* act 5, scene 7.

22. ETG to PHH, 8 October 1867 [HTP-SCL].

Chapter 12. "He had the true fire within"

1. *Daily Phoenix,* 8 October 1867; unidentified, undated newspaper clipping, [October 1867] (HTP-SCL); ETG to [Edith Goodwin], 29 October 1867 (HTP-SCL).

2. Hubbell, 96, 156–57; Sallie A. Brock, *The Southern Amaranth* (New York: Wilcox & Rockwell, 1869), 568–88; ETG to PHH, 6 November 1867 (HTP–SCL); William J. Rivers, *A Little Book: To Obtain Means for Placing a Memorial Stone upon the Grave of the Poet Henry Timrod* (Charleston: Walker, Evans & Cogswell, n. d.); ETG and KT to William J. Rivers, n. d. (HTP-SCL).

3. ETG to Mary M. Hayne, 15 October 1867 and ETG to PHH, 31 October 1867 (HTP-SCL).

4. Hubbell, 97; ETG to PHH, 31 October 1867 and 6 November 1867 (HTP-SCL).

5. ETG to PHH, 21 November 1867 and 23 November 1867 (HTP-SCL).

6. PHH to Clara Dargan, 8 January 1872 in Hubbell, 99. Hayne waited until he had a publisher before completing his "Memoir" of Timrod's life. See PHH to ————, 3 July 1873 (PHH Papers, Duke University).

7. ETG to PHH, 18 May 1870 in Hubbell, 101; WGS to ETG, 25 December 1868 (William Gilmore Simms Papers, South Caroliniana Library); WGS to John R. Thompson, 8 May 1869, in Oliphant 5: 220.

8. ETG to PHH, 4 October 1868 and 18 May 1870 (HTP-SCL); *Daily Phoenix,* 16 April 1870.

9. ETG to PHH, 4 October 1868, and PHH to ETG, 9 August 1872 (HTP-SCL).

10. ETG to PHH, 27 August 1872 and 15 September 1872 (HTP-SCL); KT to PHH, 1873 (HTP-SCL). In a letter to Clara Dargan written on 23 April 1870 Hayne has—"in the strictest confidence"—harsh words about Timrod's widow. Katie "is a trivial, foolish, shallow-brained, if not bad-hearted woman,—who married Timrod, in a freak of disappointed vanity,—made his life (tho he never complained by word or deed), unhappy, and who, I understand upon good authority, is not likely in any way to honor his memory!! Perhaps, poor dear fellow! he was taken away from the misery to come! I know not." (Hubbell, 17). Hayne's comments concerning Katie are most positive in the "Memoir," 43, and in his correspondence with her he is always cordial. Hayne and his son visited Washington in June 1873 after receiving many invitations from Katie. "Mrs. Timrod has treated us in the kindest, most hospitable fashion," he reported to his wife. See PHH to Mary M. Hayne, 22 June 1873 (PHH Papers, Duke University).

11. KT to PHH, 22 January 1873, in Hubbell, 103; unidentified, undated [October 1872] newspaper clipping in scrapbook (HTP-SCL).

12. Edwin Perry Whipple to PHH, 10 March 1875 (Edwin Perry Whipple Papers, Alderman Library); Daniel Morley McKeithan, ed., *A Collection of Hayne Let-*

ters (Austin: University of Texas Press, 1944), 318–19; PHH to Edward Spencer, 28 February 1873 (Paul Hamilton Hayne Letters, Alderman Library).

13. John Greenleaf Whittier to PHH, 17 March 1870, in John B. Pickard, ed., *The Letters of John Greenleaf Whittier* 3 (Cambridge: Belknap Press of Harvard University Press, 1975), 220; ETG to PHH, 18 May 1870, in Hubbell, 112.

14. PHH to John Greenleaf Whittier, 23 March 1870 in John Albree, ed., *Whittier Correspondence From the Oak Knoll Collections, 1830–1892* (Salem: Essex Book and Print Club, 1911), 176; John Greenleaf Whittier to PHH, 2 May 1873, in Hubbell, 117–18; Oliver Wendell Holmes to PHH, 24 January 1873 (PHH Papers, Duke University).

15. PHH to Rossiter Johnson, 10 October 1876, in Hubbell, 104–105.

16. PHH to Sidney Lanier, 25 July 1877, in Rayburn S. Moore, ed., *A Man of Letters in the Nineteenth Century South: Selected Letters of Paul Hamilton Hayne* (Baton Rouge: Louisiana State University Press, 1982), 145; Charles R. Anderson, ed., *The Centennial Edition of the Works of Sidney Lanier.* 10 vols. Volume 6: *Florida and Miscellaneous Prose* (Baltimore: The Johns Hopkins University Press, 1945), xviii–xix, 160–61.

17. PHH to Henry Wadsworth Longfellow, n. d., in McKeithan, ed., *Hayne Letters,* 150; *News and Courier,* 28 June 1896.

18. William A. Courtenay to Henry Timrod Goodwin, 21 November 1898 (HTP-SCL); Charles H. Ross to Richard Henry Stoddard, 26 February 1894 (Charles Hunter Ross Papers, Alderman Library); "Henry Timrod Memorial Fund" coupon, 1896 (HTP-SCL). Courtenay and Hayne had been bitter rivals from at least 1862. See PHH to Mary M. Hayne, 28 February 1862 (PHH Papers, Duke University).

19. "The Timrod Revival," n. d., pamphlet enclosed with ms. 4 (Herbert Baxter Adams Collection, The Milton S. Eisenhower Library); William A. Courtenay to ———, 18 September 1899 (HTP-SCL). Timrod's grave in Trinity churchyard remained unmarked for over a decade. In 1879 Hugh Thompson, by then South Carolina's superintendent of education, led a modest fund-raising effort that brought in enough money to erect a marble monument. The present monument lists 1829 as Timrod's year of birth, the correct year—1828—not having been discovered until 1935. Markers were also erected for his mother and his sister "Edyth," an alternate spelling seldom if ever used in her lifetime.

20. Note by William A. Courtenay, n. d., and Rachel Lyons Heustis to William A. Courtenay, 20 March 1899 and 29 August 1900 (William A. Courtenay Papers, South Caroliniana Library).

21. Katie Timrod Lloyd to William A. Courtenay, 23 May 1899 (William A. Courtenay Papers, South Caroliniana Library); statement of William A. Courtenay, 7 October 1902 (William A. Courtenay Papers, South Caroliniana Library); clipping from *State* newspaper, n. d. [March 1913] (HTP-SCL).

22. "Notes and Queries—Timrod," *South Carolina Historical and Genealogical Magazine* 2 (1901): 250. The concluding phrase quotes Acts 26:19.

Bibliography

Manuscripts

Herbert Baxter Adams. Collection. The Milton S. Eisenhower Library, Johns Hopkins University, Baltimore, Md.

A. W. Anthony. Collection. Manuscripts and Archives Section, New York Public Library, New York, N. Y.

Beaufort District, S. C. Census of 1860. U. S. National Archives, Washington, D. C.

Case files for applications from former Confederates for Presidential pardons, South Carolina. U. S. National Archives, Washington, D. C.

Charleston District, S. C. Census of 1850. U. S. National Archives, Washington, D. C.

Colleton District, S. C. Census of 1850. U. S. National Archives, Washington, D. C.

William A. Courtenay. Papers. South Caroliniana Library, University of South Carolina, Columbia, S. C.

William A. Courtenay. Collection. Charleston Library Society, Charleston, S. C.

Darlington District, S. C. Census of 1850. U. S. National Archives, Washington, D. C.

General Index, Miscellaneous Records of Bills of Sale, 1729–1825. South Carolina Department of Archives and History, Columbia, S. C.

Paul Hamilton Hayne. Papers. Alderman Library, University of Virginia, Charlottesville, Va.

Paul Hamilton Hayne. Papers. Special Collections Library, Duke University, Durham, NC.

Ladies' Association to Commemorate the Confederate Dead. Program, 1866. South Caroliniana Library, University of South Carolina, Columbia, S. C.

Thomas Ollive Mabbott. Collection. Harry Ransom Humanities Research Center, The University of Texas at Austin.

William Gordon McCabe. Papers. Alderman Library, University of Virginia, Charlottesville, Va.

Orangeburgh District, S. C. Census of 1850. U. S. National Archives, Washington, D. C.

Orangeburgh District, S. C. Census of 1860. U. S. National Archives, Washington, D. C.

Richland District, S. C. Census of 1860. U. S. National Archives, Washington, D. C.

William James Rivers. Papers. South Caroliniana Library, University of South Carolina, Columbia, S. C.

Charles Hunter Ross. Papers. Alderman Library, University of Virginia, Charlottesville, Va.

William Gilmore Simms. Papers. South Caroliniana Library, University of South Carolina, Columbia, S. C.

Sosnowski Family. Scrapbook. South Caroliniana Library, University of South Carolina, Columbia, S. C.

Sosnowski-Schaller Families. Papers. South Caroliniana Library, University of South Carolina, Columbia, S. C.

South Carolina Volunteers, 20th Regiment, Co. B. Muster Roll and Pay Roll, 1 July–31 August 1862. South Caroliniana Library, University of South Carolina, Columbia, S. C.

Richard Henry Stoddard. Papers. Alderman Library, University of Virginia, Charlottesville, Va.

John R. Thompson. Papers. Alderman Library, University of Virginia, Charlottesville, Va.

Henry Timrod. Letters (Collection C10199). Department of Rare Books and Special Collections, Princeton University Library, Princeton University, Princeton, N. J.

Henry Timrod. Papers. Alderman Library, University of Virginia, Charlottesville, Va.

Henry Timrod. Papers. Compiled Service Records of Confederate Soldiers Who Served in Organizations from the State of South Carolina. U. S. National Archives, Washington, D. C.

Henry Timrod. Papers. South Caroliniana Library, University of South Carolina, Columbia, S. C.

William Henry Timrod. Papers. South Carolina Historical Society, Charleston, S. C.

Edwin Percy Whipple. Papers. Alderman Library, University of Virginia, Charlottesville, Va.

William H. Wills. Papers. Southern Historical Collection, University of North Carolina, Chapel Hill, N. C.

NEWSPAPERS

Athens Herald [Athens, Georgia], 1917.

City Gazette and Commercial Daily Advertiser [Charleston], 1828.

Daily Courier [Charleston], 1866.

Daily Phoenix [Columbia], 1866, 1867, 1870.

Daily South Carolinian [Columbia and Charleston], 1864, 1865, 1866.

News and Courier [Charleston], 1896, 1899, 1901, 1903.

Southern Banner [Athens, Georgia], 1845, 1846.

The Southron [Orangeburg, South Carolina], 1856.

The State [Columbia], 1913.

Published Primary Sources

Albree, John, ed. *Whittier Correspondence from the Oak Knoll Collections, 1830–1892.* Salem: Essex Book and Print Club, 1911.

Altman, Peggy B., et al., compilers. *1850 Census of Darlington County, South Carolina.* N. p.: privately printed, n. d.

Anderson, Charles R., ed. *The Centennial Edition of the Works of Sidney Lanier.* 10 volumes. Volume 6: *Florida and Miscellaneous Prose,* edited by Philip Graham, ed. Baltimore: The Johns Hopkins Press, 1945.

Austin, Henry, Carl McKinley and William A. Courtenay. *Timrod Souvenir.* Aiken, S. C.: The Palmetto Press, 1901.

Becker, Kate Harbes. *Paul Hamilton Hayne: Life and Letters.* Belmont, N. C.: The Outline Company, 1951.

Bernhard, Duke of Saxe–Weimar–Eisenach. *Travels by His Highness Duke Bernhard of Saxe–Weimar–Eisenach through North America in the Years 1825 and 1826.* Translated by William Jeronimus. Edited by C. J. Jeronimus. Lanham, Md.: University Press of America, 2001.

Briggs, Ward W., Jr., ed. *The Letters of Basil Lanneau Gildersleeve.* Baltimore: The Johns Hopkins University Press, 1987.

De Leon, T. C. *Belles, Beaux, and Brains of the '60's.* New York: G. W. Dillingham Co., 1907.

"Editorial note." *The Living Age,* no. 878, 30 March 1861.

Fidler, William, ed. "Notes and Documents." *The Alabama Review* 2 (April 1949).

———. "Unpublished Letters of Henry Timrod." *Southern Literary Messenger* 2 (October, November, December, 1940).

Gildersleeve, Basil L. "Formative Influences." *The Forum,* February 1891.

Hagy, James W., ed. *City Directories for Charleston, South Carolina for the Years 1803, 1806, 1807, 1809 and 1813.* Baltimore: Clearfield Co., 1995.

Hayne, Paul Hamilton. "Ante-Bellum Charleston." *The Southern Bivouac* 1: 6 (November 1885).

Hewett, Janet B., ed. *Supplement to the Official Records of the Union and Confederate Armies.* 100 volumes. Wilmington, N. C.: Broadfoot Publishing Company, 1998.

Holcomb, Brent, compiler, *South Carolina Marriages, 1688–1799.* Baltimore: Genealogical Publishing Co., 1980.

Hubbell, Jay B., ed. *The Last Years of Henry Timrod 1864–1867.* Durham: Duke University Press, 1941.

Journal of the House of Representatives of the State of South Carolina Being the Regular Session of 1866. Columbia: F. G. De Fontaine, State Printer, 1866.

Kane, Elisha Kent. *Arctic Explorations: The Second Grinnell Expedition in Search of Sir John Franklin.* Philadelphia: Childs & Peterson, 1856.

"Literary Notices," *Harper's New Monthly Magazine,* 20, no. 117 (February 1860).

Mabbott, Thomas Ollive, ed. "Some Letters of Henry Timrod." *The American Collector* 3 (February 1927).

McKeithan, Daniel Morley, ed. *A Collection of Hayne Letters.* Austin: The University of Texas Press, 1944.

————. "Paul Hamilton Hayne Writes to the Granddaughter of Patrick Henry," *Georgia Historical Quarterly* 30, no. 1 (March 1948).

Moore, Caroline T., comp. and ed. *Abstracts of Wills of Charleston District, South Carolina 1783–1800.* Columbia: R. L. Bryan Co., 1974.

Moore, Rayburn S., ed. *A Man of Letters in the Nineteenth-Century South: Selected Letters of Paul Hamilton Hayne.* Baton Rouge: Louisiana State University Press, 1982.

Oliphant, Mary C. Simms, Alfred Taylor Odell, T.C. Duncan Eaves, eds. *The Letters of William Gilmore Simms.* 6 volumes. Columbia: University of South Carolina Press, 1955–1982.

Pickard, John B., ed. *The Letters of John Greenleaf Whittier.* Cambridge: Belknap Press of Harvard University Press, 1975.

"Poll Lists, Charleston Municipal Elections, 1787." *South Carolina Historical Magazine* 56 (1955).

"Register of the Independent Congregational (Circular) Church of Charleston, South Carolina." *South Carolina Historical and Genealogical Magazine* 33 (1932).

Rivers, William J. *A Little Book: To Obtain Means for Placing a Memorial Stone Upon the Grave of the Poet Henry Timrod.* Charleston: Walker, Evans & Cogswell, n. d.

Ross, Fitzgerald. *A Visit to the Cities and Camps of the Confederate States.* London: W. Blackwood, 1865.

Salley, A. S., Jr., ed. and comp. *Marriage Notices in the South-Carolina Gazette and its Successors 1732–1801.* Baltimore: Genealogical Publishing Co., 1965.

Selby, Julian A. *Memorabilia and Anecdotal Reminiscences of Columbia, South Carolina.* Columbia: The R. L. Bryan Company, 1905.

Sturgill, Claude C. and Charles L. Prince. "McCabe's Impression of the Bombardment of Charleston, 1863." *South Carolina Historical Magazine* 71 (1970).

Timrod, Henry. *Katie.* New York: E. J. Hale, 1884.

————. *Poems of Henry Timrod.* Boston: Houghton Mifflin, 1899. Reprinted Richmond: B. F. Johnson, 1901.

————. *Poems.* Boston: Ticknor and Fields, 1859.

————. *The Collected Poems of Henry Timrod: A Variorum Edition.* Edited by Edd Winfield Parks and Aileen Wells Parks. Athens: University of Georgia Press, 1965.

————. *The Essays of Henry Timrod.* Edited by Edd Winfield Parks. Athens: University of Georgia Press, 1942.

————. *The Poems of Henry Timrod.* Edited by Paul Hamilton Hayne. New York: E. J. Hale & Son, 1873.

————. *The Uncollected Poems of Henry Timrod.* Edited by Guy A. Cardwell, Jr. Athens: University of Georgia Press, 1942.

————. *Verses From the Cotton Boll: Official Souvenir of the Woman's Department of the South Carolina Interstate and West Indian Exposition, Charleston, South Carolina, USA, 1901–1902.* Boston: Stillings Press, 1901.

Timrod Memorial Association. *Proceedings at the Unveiling of the Art Memorial in Washington Square, Charleston, South Carolina, May–Day, 1901.* Charleston: Lucas & Richardson Co., n. d.

Timrod, William Henry. "Scene From an Unpublished Drama." *Southern Literary Journal* 1, no. 4 (December 1835).

———. "Scene From an Unpublished Drama." *The Southern Rose* 5, no. 25 (5 August 1837).

Vizetelly, Henry. *Glances Back Through Seventy Years: Autobiographical and Other Reminiscences.* 2 volumes. London: Kegan, Paul, Trench & Co., 1893.

Wauchope, George Armstrong. "Henry Timrod: Man and Poet, A Critical Study." *Bulletin of the University of South Carolina* 41, part 4 (April 1915).

Webber, Mabel L., comp. "Marriage and Death Notices From the South Carolina Weekly Gazette." *The South Carolina Historical and Genealogical Magazine* 19 (1918).

Woodward, C. Vann, ed. *Mary Chesnut's Civil War.* New Haven: Yale University Press, 1981.

Unpublished Studies

Loney, James Randolph. "The Poetry and Poetics of Henry Timrod, Paul Hamilton Hayne, and Sidney Lanier: An Essay on Art and Community in the Nineteenth-Century South." PhD dissertation, University of Georgia, 1977.

Long, Edgar. "Russell's Magazine as an Expression of Ante-Bellum South Carolina Culture." PhD dissertation, University of South Carolina, 1932.

West, William Franciscus, Jr. "A Southern Editor Views the Civil War: A Collection of Editorials by Henry Timrod and Other Editorial Materials Published in the *Daily South Carolinian,* January 14, 1864, to February 17, 1865." PhD dissertation, Florida State University, 1984.

Secondary Sources

Brock, Sallie A. *The Southern Amaranth.* New York: Wilcox & Rockwell, 1869.

Burton, E. Milby. *The Siege of Charleston, 1861–1865.* Columbia: University of South Carolina Press, 1970.

Capers, Ellison. *Confederate Military History Extended Edition.* Volume VI: *South Carolina.* Wilmington, N. C.: Broadfoot Publishing Co, 1987.

Cardwell, Guy A., Jr. "The Date of Henry Timrod's Birth." *American Literature* 7 (May 1935).

———. "William Henry Timrod, the Charleston Volunteers, and the Defense of St. Augustine." *The North Carolina Historical Review* 18, no. 1 (January 1941).

Chisolm, William Garnett. *Chisolm Genealogy.* New York: The Knickerbocker Press, 1914.

Cisco, Walter Brian. *Taking a Stand: Portraits From the Southern Secession Movement.* Shippensburg, Pa.: White Mane Books, 1998.

———. *Wade Hampton: Confederate Warrior, Conservative Statesman.* Dulles, Va.: Brassey's, Inc., 2004.

Clare, Virginia Pettigrew. *Harp of the South.* Atlanta: Oglethorpe University Press, 1936.

Congaware, George J. *The History of the German Friendly Society of Charleston, South Carolina, 1766–1916.* Richmond: Garrett & Massie, Publishers, 1935.

Corner, George W. *Doctor Kane of the Arctic Seas.* Philadelphia: Temple University Press, 1972.

Coulter, E. Merton. *College Life in the Old South.* Athens: University of Georgia Press, 1983.

Culler, Daniel Marchant. *Orangeburgh District, 1768–1868: History and Records.* Spartanburg, S. C.: The Reprint Company, 1995.

Davis, William C. *"A Government of Our Own:" The Making of the Confederacy.* New York: The Free Press, 1994.

De Bellis, Jack. *Sidney Lanier, Henry Timrod, and Paul Hamilton Hayne: A Reference Guide.* Boston: G. K. Hall & Co., 1978.

Dormandy, Thomas. *The White Death: A History of Tuberculosis.* New York: New York University Press, 2000.

Dyer, Thomas G. *The University of Georgia: A Bicentennial History, 1785–1985.* Athens: University of Georgia Press, 1985.

Fellman, Michael. *Citizen Sherman: A Life of William Tecumseh Sherman.* New York: Random House, 1995.

Foote, Shelby. *The Civil War: A Narrative.* Volume 1: *Fort Sumter to Perryville.* New York: Vintage Books, 1986.

Freehling, William H. *Prelude to Civil War: The Nullification Controversy in South Carolina 1816–1836.* New York: Oxford University Press, 1966.

Gordon, Armistead Churchill. *Memories and Memorials of William Gordon McCabe.* Richmond: Old Dominion Press, 1925.

Green, Edwin L. *A History of the University of South Carolina.* Columbia: The State Company, 1916.

Guilds, John Caldwell. *Simms: A Literary Life.* Fayetteville: University of Arkansas Press, 1992.

Hargrett, Lester. "Student Life at the University of Georgia in the 1840s," *The Georgia Historical Quarterly* 8, no. 1 (March 1924).

History of the Synod Committee. *A History of the Lutheran Church in South Carolina.* Columbia: R. L. Bryan Company, 1971.

Hollis, Daniel Walker. *University of South Carolina.* Volume 1: *South Carolina College.* Columbia: University of South Carolina Press, 1951.

Hoole, W. Stanley. *Vizetelly Covers the Confederacy.* Tuscaloosa, Ala.: Confederate Publishing Company, 1957.

Mahon, John K. *History of the Second Seminole War, 1835–1842.* Gainesville: University of Florida Press, 1985.

Meriwether, Colyer. *History of Higher Education in South Carolina With a Sketch of the Free School System.* Washington: Government Printing Office, 1889.

Moore, Rayburn S. *Paul Hamilton Hayne.* New York: Twayne Publishers, 1972.

"Notes and Queries—Timrod," *South Carolina Historical and Genealogical Magazine* 2 (1901).

Parks, Edd Winfield. *Henry Timrod.* New York: Twayne Publishers, 1964.

————. "Timrod's College Days," *American Literature,* 7 (November 1936).

Rogers, George C., Jr. *Charleston in the Age of the Pinckneys.* Norman: University of Oklahoma Press, 1969.

Rowland, Lawrence S., Alexander Moore, and George C. Rogers, Jr. *The History of Beaufort County, South Carolina.* Volume 1: *1514–1861.* Columbia: University of South Carolina Press, 1996.

Salley, A. S., Jr. *The History of Orangeburg County South Carolina.* Baltimore: Regional Publishing Company, 1978.

Seigler, Milledge B. "Henry Timrod and Sophie Sosnowski." *The Georgia Historical Quarterly* 31, no. 3 (September 1947).

Snowden, Yates. *History of South Carolina.* 5 volumes. Chicago: Lewis Publishing Co., 1920.

Sondley, F. A. *A History of Buncombe County, North Carolina.* Spartanburg, S. C.: The Reprint Company, 1977.

Sprague, John T. *The Origin, Progress, and Conclusion of the Florida War.* New York: D. Appleton & Company, 1848.

Taylor, Rupert. "Henry Timrod's Ancestress, Hannah Caesar," *American Literature* 9 (January 1938).

Thomas, Albert Sidney. *A Historical Account of the Protestant Episcopal Church in South Carolina 1820–1957.* Columbia: R. L. Bryan Co., 1957.

Thompson, Henry T. *Henry Timrod: Laureate of the Confederacy.* Columbia: The State Company, 1928.

Towles, Louis P., ed. *A World Turned Upside Down: The Palmers of South Santee, 1818–1881.* Columbia: University of South Carolina Press, 1996.

Trent, William P. *William Gilmore Simms.* Boston: Houghton, Mifflin and Company, 1892.

Vaughan, Richard. *The Arctic: A History.* Gloucestershire: Alan Sutton Publishing Limited, 1994.

Voigt, G. P. "New Light on Timrod's 'Memorial Ode,'" *American Literature* 4 (January 1933).

Wade, John Donald. *Augustus Baldwin Longstreet: A Study of the Development of Culture in the South.* New York: Macmillan Company, 1924.

Index

Note: Page numbers in italics are illustrations.